Guitar Folksong Duets
For Pupil and Teacher

By Adrian Allan

Edited by Allan H. Jones

Cover design by Phil Ogden

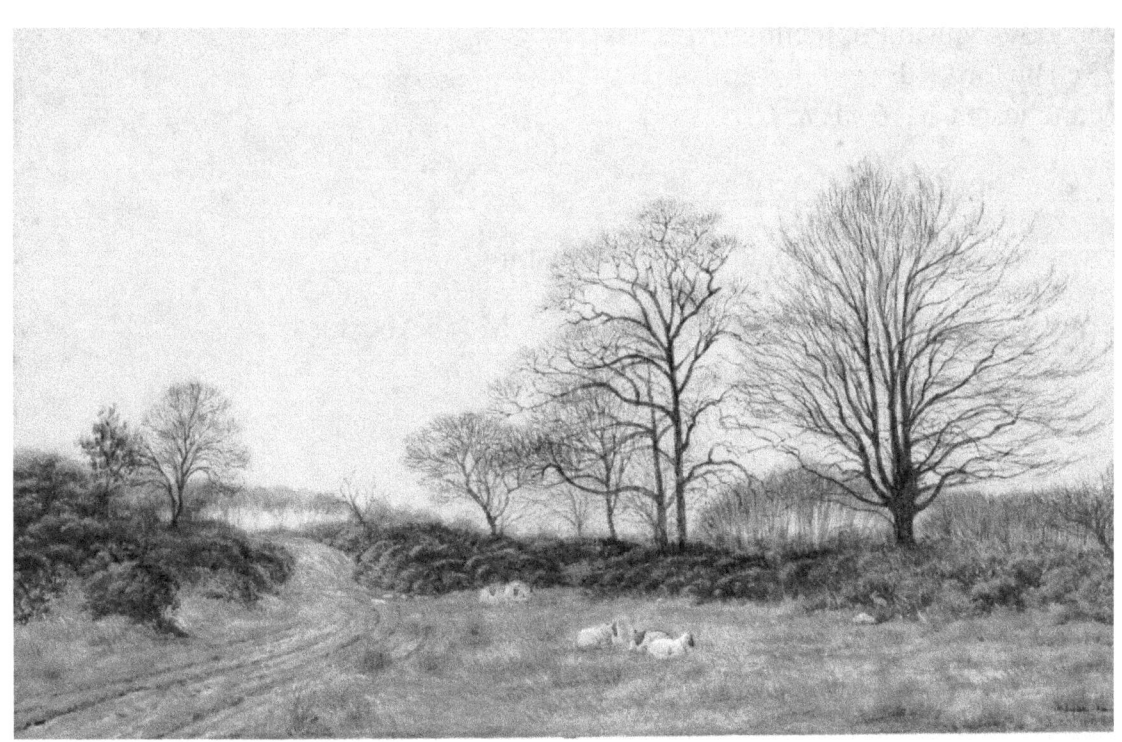

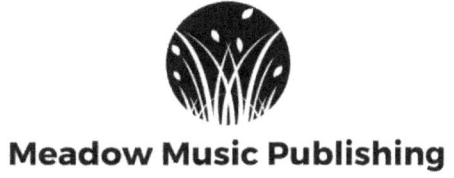

Meadow Music Publishing

Second Edition: 2018

Meadow Music Publishing
23c Burford Rd
Manchester, M16 8EW

www.juliealford@btinternet.com.

www.facebook.com/meadowmusicpublishing/

Front cover illustration by J. Wager: Hook Moor Aberford

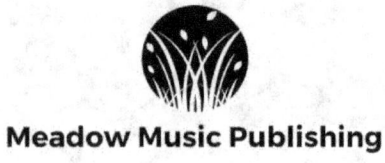

Meadow Music Publishing

Contents

Preface

From the early 1990s the main exam boards started to offer early-grade pupils the option of choosing to play a duet with their teachers, as an alternative to solo guitar playing, which could be quite intimidating for young pupils. The duet approach was also lauded by John Williams, amongst others, as a way of introducing ensemble skills to guitarists from an early age.

However well-intentioned this approach might have been, it was never supported by a set of well arranged and playable teacher and pupil duets. The first publications were effective in parts, but suffered from the inclusion of pieces that were either poorly arranged, or were, in themselves, original pieces that were written in a modern style, often leaving the pupil (and often the teacher) feeling rather cold.

This book hopes to fill a long standing gap. It offers a selection of pieces that have proved their worth over the passage of time; they are melodic, memorable and timeless in their appeal to all ages. The aim was to come up with arrangements that are simple for the early stage pupil (around grades 1-3) but offer a musically satisfying experience for the teacher, as well.

The pupil parts only once venture above fret five (a solitary B on string one, fret seven) and are never in keys of more than two sharps or one flat. The teacher parts explore various musical techniques to support the melodies, such as contrary motion, chord substitutions, secondary dominants and scordatura. The melody lines can also be played by other instruments in C such as recorder and flute. More advanced, or at least, intermediate players, can attempt to play the teacher parts.

It might be noted that there are no repeats (with only one exception in the book); the teacher and pupil will agree on a set number of verses. There are also no fingerings in the book. The pupil parts are all very limited to the first three positions, and the teacher should be able to work out the guitar parts.

A note on the music

Information about the tunes has been included, where space permitted. However, here is a little background on the remainder:

Allan Water is believed to have been written by Matthew Lewis (1775-1818), the English author, best known for his gothic novel 'The Monk'. The song refers to a Scottish river. The song became very popular and features in Thomas Hardy's 1874 novel 'Far From the Madding Crowd'.

The Lincolnshire Poacher is considered the unofficial anthem of the county of Lincolnshire. It was first published around 1776 and is said to have been a favourite of King George IV. It is also used as march by the Royal Lincolnshire Regiment.

An Eriskay Love Lilt is absolute proof that the most simple of songs can be the most beautiful. Eriskay is an island of only three square miles in the south of the Outer Hebrides chain. In 1745 Bonnie Prince Charlie stepped foot on its soil before launching the Jacobite Rebellion. It is said that the pink campion that grows on the island fell from his handkerchief. The whole piece, harmonics included, is to be played *molto gentile* and *semplice*.

Cockles and Mussels is the story of a fishmonger, Molly Malone, who plied her trade on the streets of Dublin, before succumbing to a fatal fever at a young age. It may not be a true "folk song" of the oral tradition, as it only appears to date back to 1883, but may be based on an earlier melody. In 1998 a bronze statue of Molly Malone was unveiled in Dublin by the Lord Mayor during the city's Millennium celebrations.

The Boar's Head Carol is named after the practice from the fifteenth century to present the head of a boar at a Christmas banquet. The head was possibly not eaten, but was ceremonial. The song was probably sung to accompany the ritual.

Land of My Fathers is the national anthem of Wales. The words were written by Evan James and the lyrics were by his son, James James. It was written in 1856 and became popular after the Llangollen festival of 1858. In 1905 it became the first anthem to be sung at a sporting event, at the *Home Nations Rugby Championship* when Wales played against New Zealand.

Drink to Me Only is an old English song. The lyrics are taken from Ben Johnson's poem, Song to Celia, from 1616. It has remained popular ever since, and was sung by such greats as Bing Crosby and Paul Robeson.

The Leaving of Liverpool was first collected on the east coast of America around 1938. It is a lament about leaving Liverpool behind and travelling to California. The singer pledges to return to his "own true love" one day. It has been a staple of the folk scene and has been recorded by many groups and artists, including Bob Dylan, The Dubliners and The Pogues.

Henry Martin is a Scottish ballad from the central lowlands. The real name of Henry Martin was Andrew Barton, a pirate who sailed a ship called *The Lion*. Henry VIII ordered the capture of Andrew Barton, who was fatally wounded. The ballad tells of his exploits.

Annie Laurie is a Romeo and Juliet style romance about lovers in rival Scottish clans. The song first came to print in 1835 and was popular with Scottish soldiers during the Crimean War.

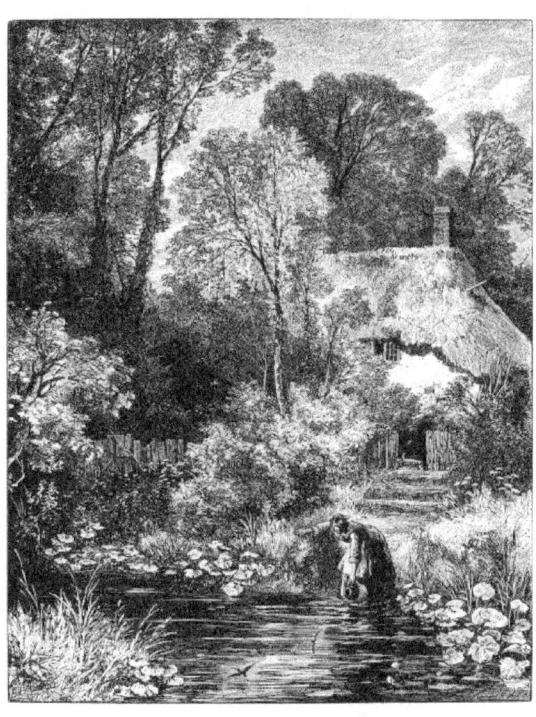

Londonderry Air
Danny Boy

Old Irish Air

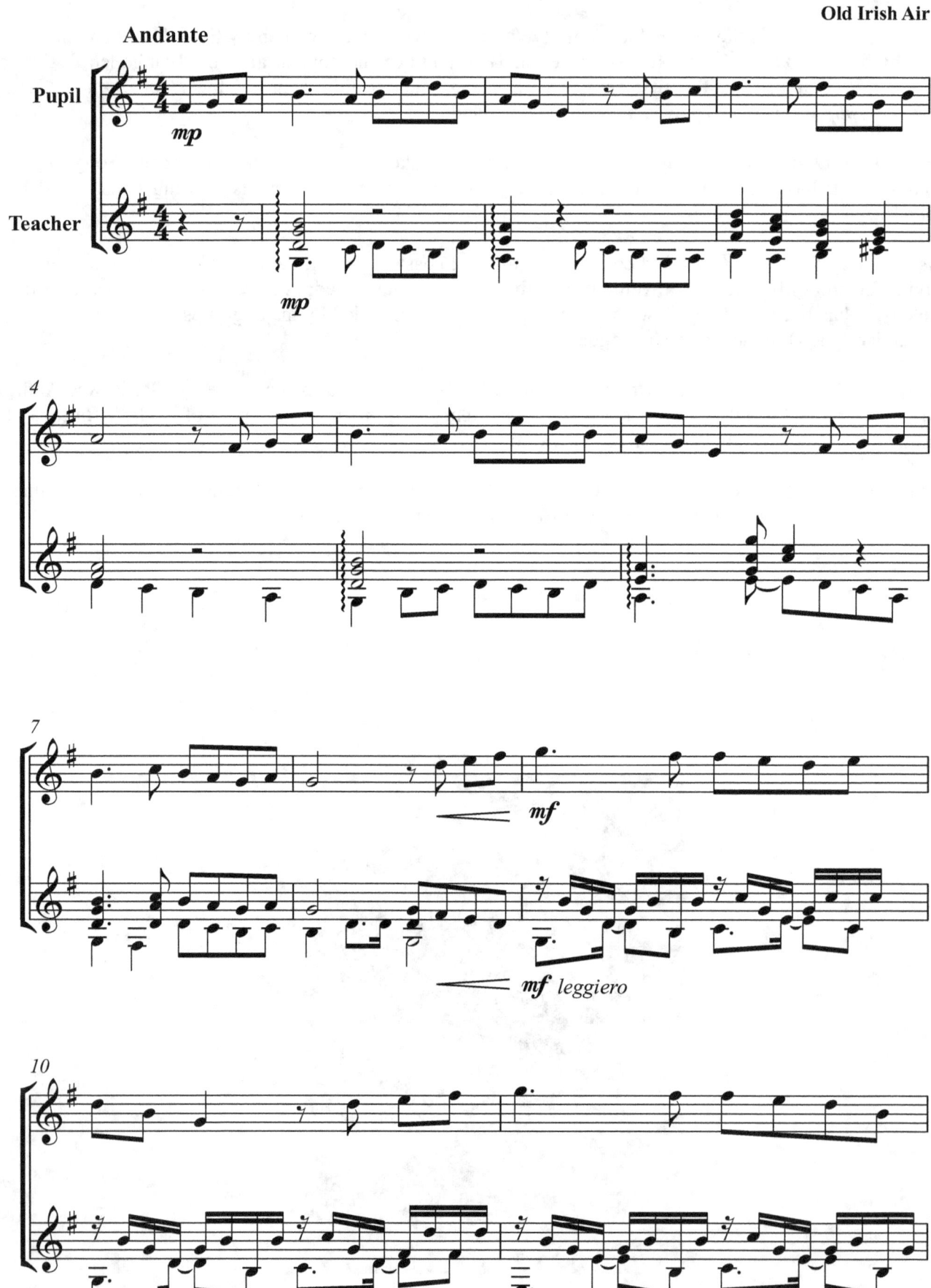

1

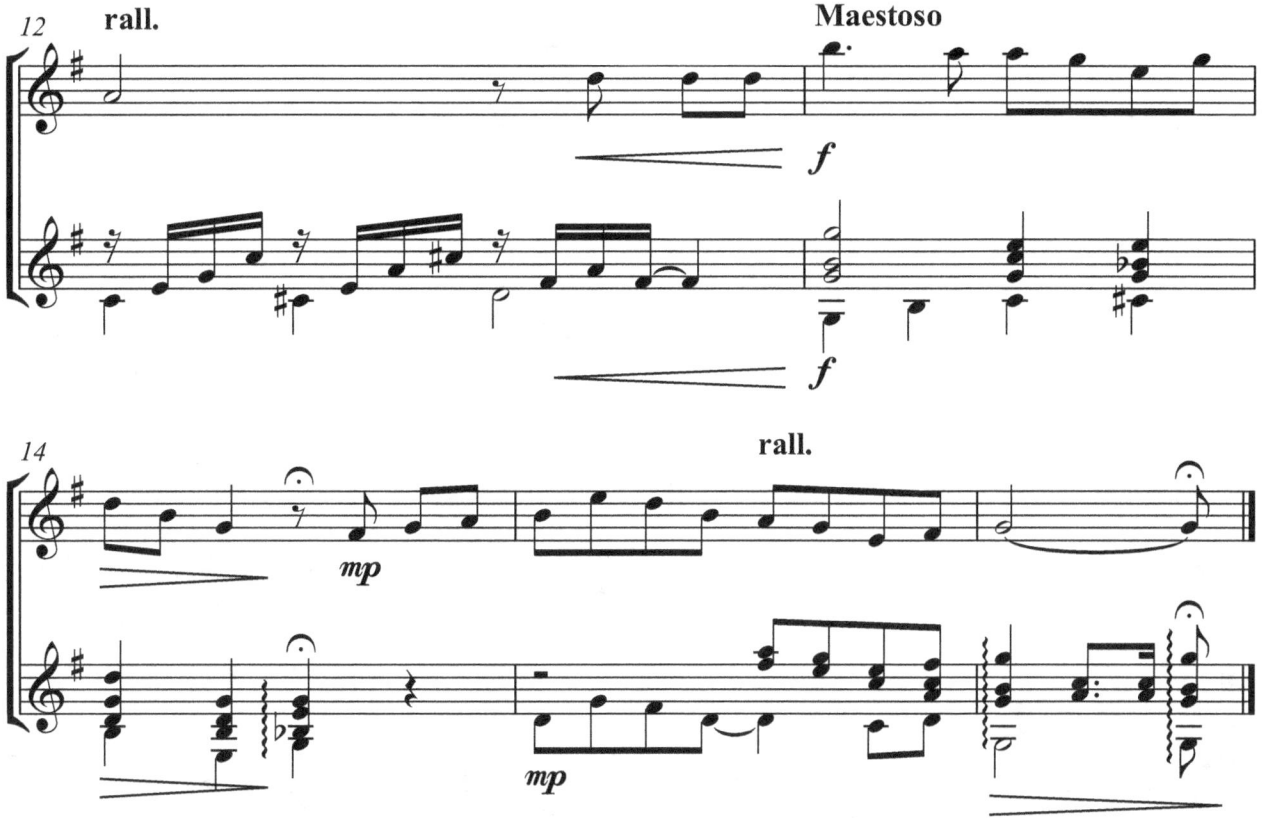

This, most famous of Irish songs was first collected in Londonderry and included in the collection "The Ancient Music of Ireland" in 1855. The words "Danny Boy" were only added in 1913, when it was set to the words of Frederick Edward Wetherly.

Throughout his career, the great Irish tenor John McCormack insisted that it be known as "Londonderry Air" on his concert programmes.

Performance note:

Do not accent the bass notes in the teacher part from bars 9 to 11.
This will turn a gentle Irish air into a rhumba rhythm!

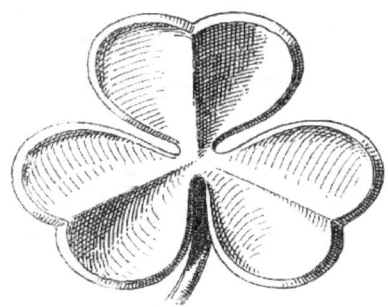

Down By the Sally Gardens

Irish Traditional

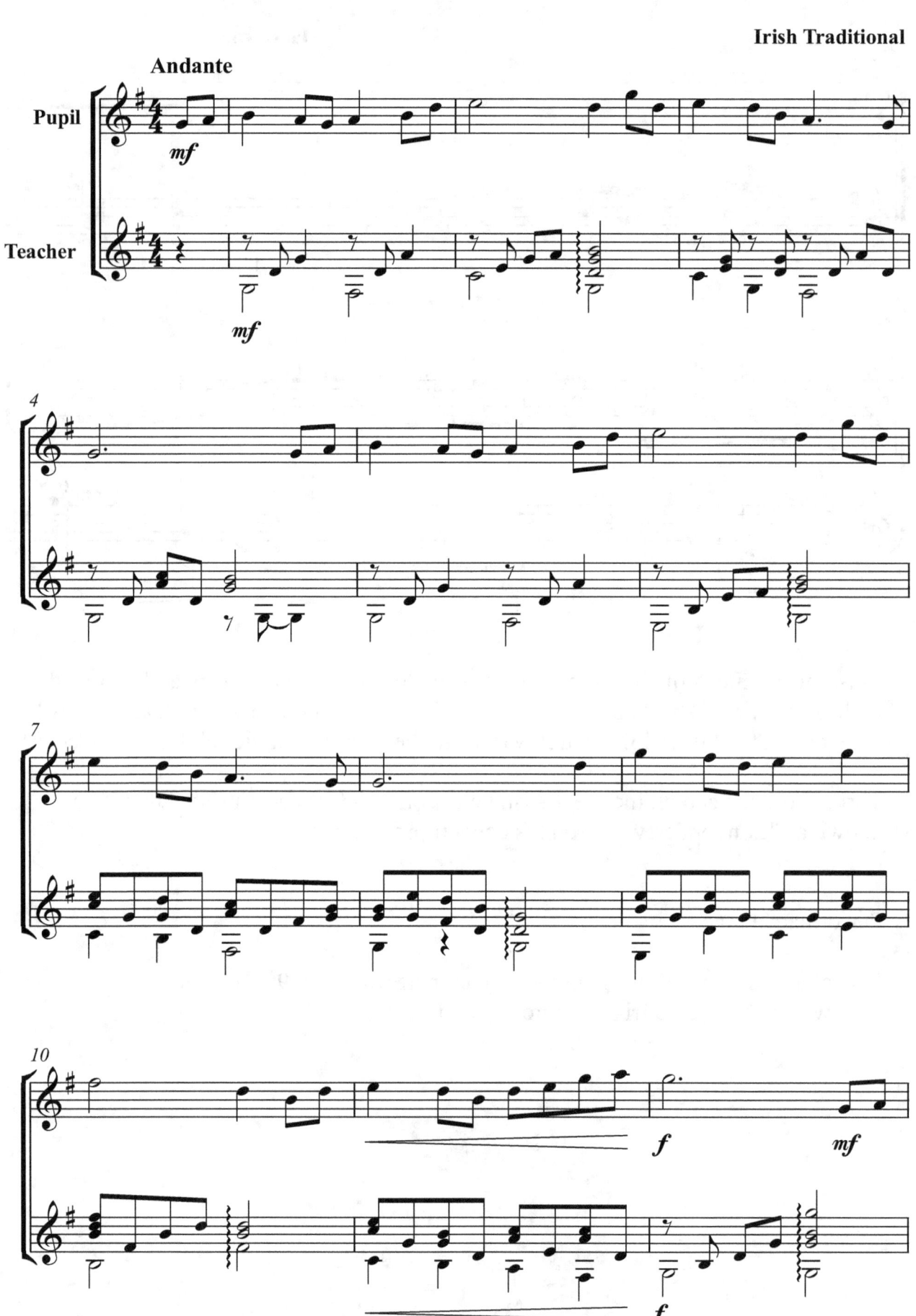

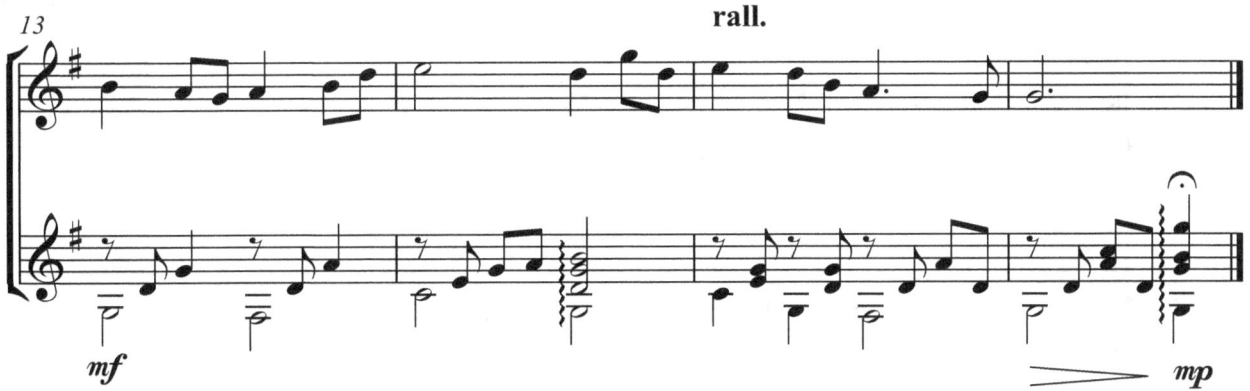

The words for this popular ballad were written by the Irish poet
W.B Yeats in 1889. The folk song scholar, Herbert Hughes, set it
to an old Irish melody.

"Sally" comes from the Gaelic word for"willow", so "sally gardens",
 are willow gardens.

Ye Banks and Braes

Scottish Air

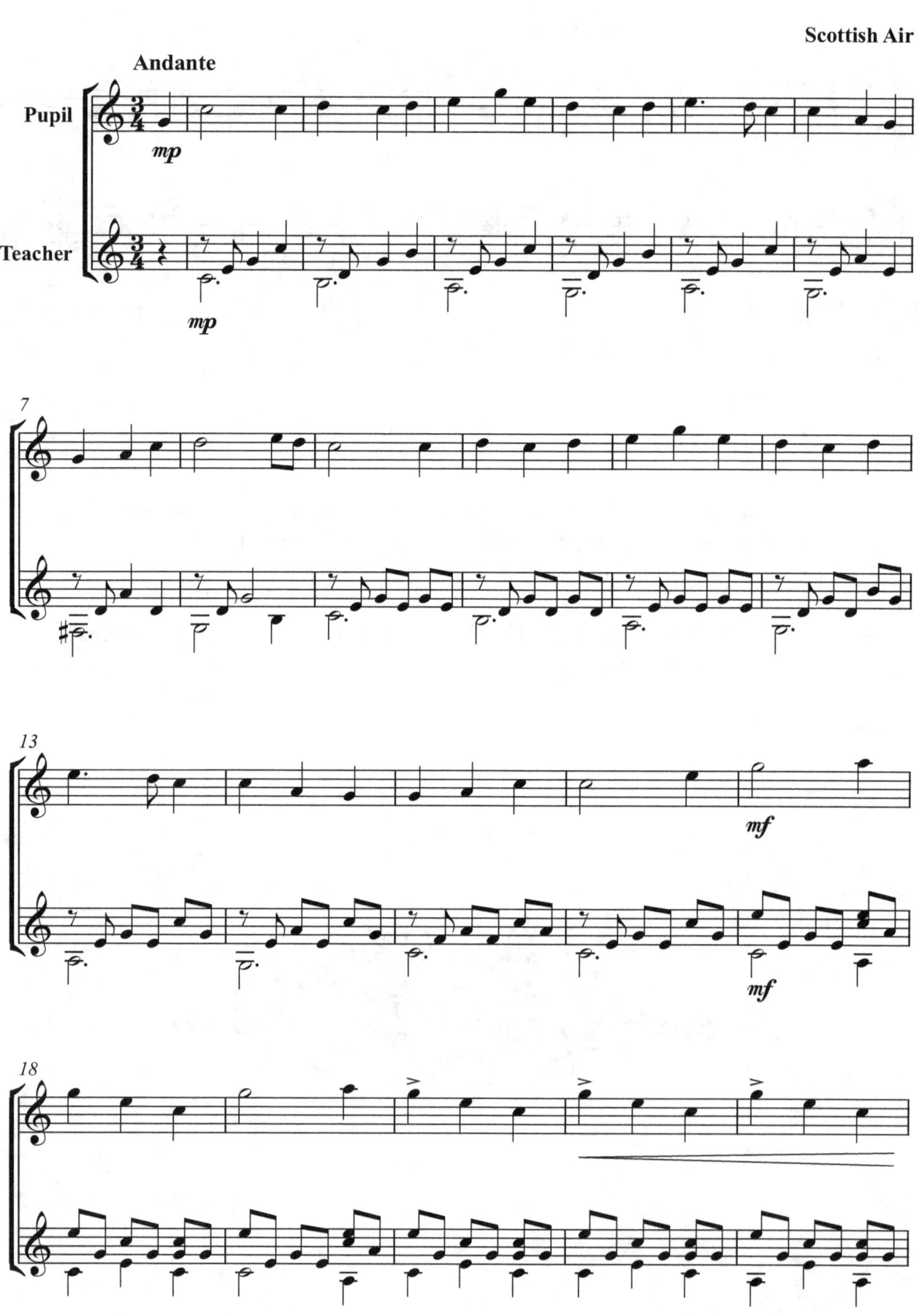

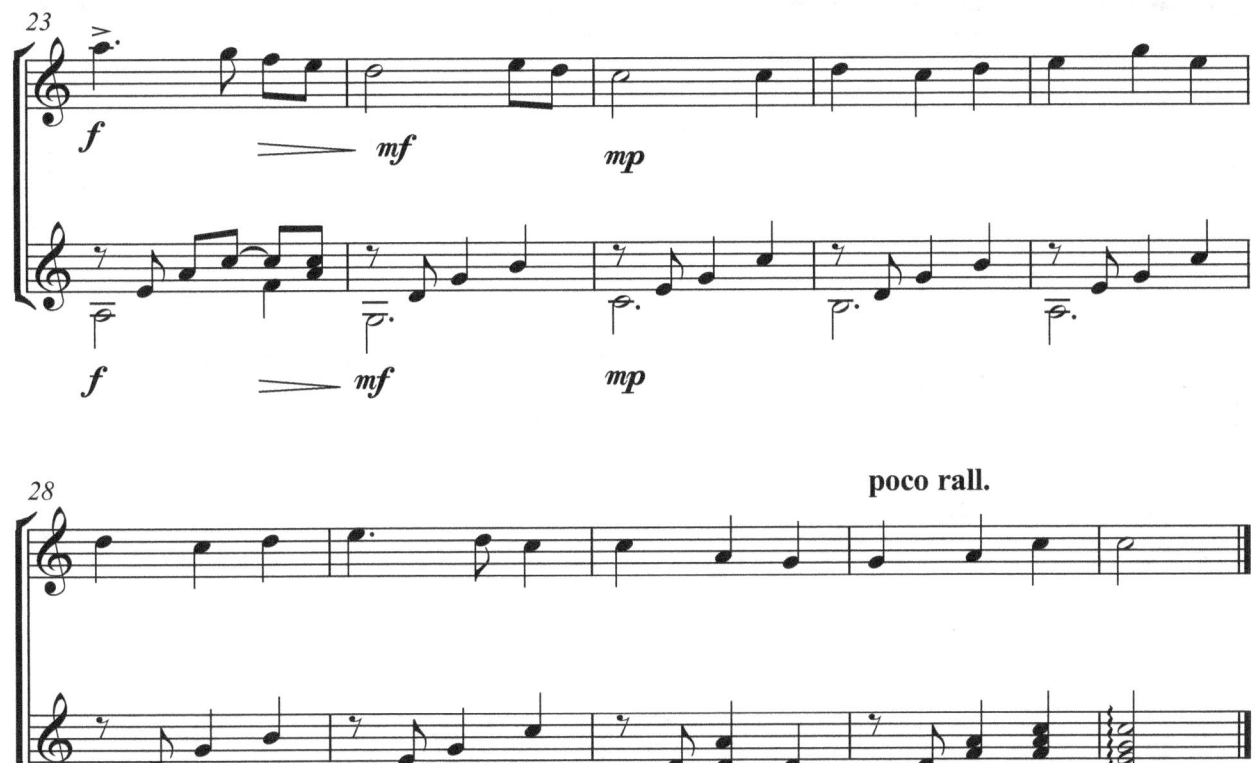

This tune was supposedly written in 1788 by Charles Miller, in response to a challenge to produce an authentic Scottish Air.

The melody was passed to Robert Burns who produced a setting that referred to "The Bonnie Doon", which is a river that passes through Burns' home town of Alloway, in Ayrshire.

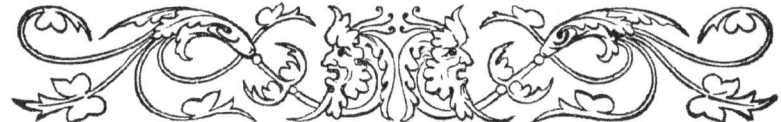

The Lincolnshire Poacher

English Traditional

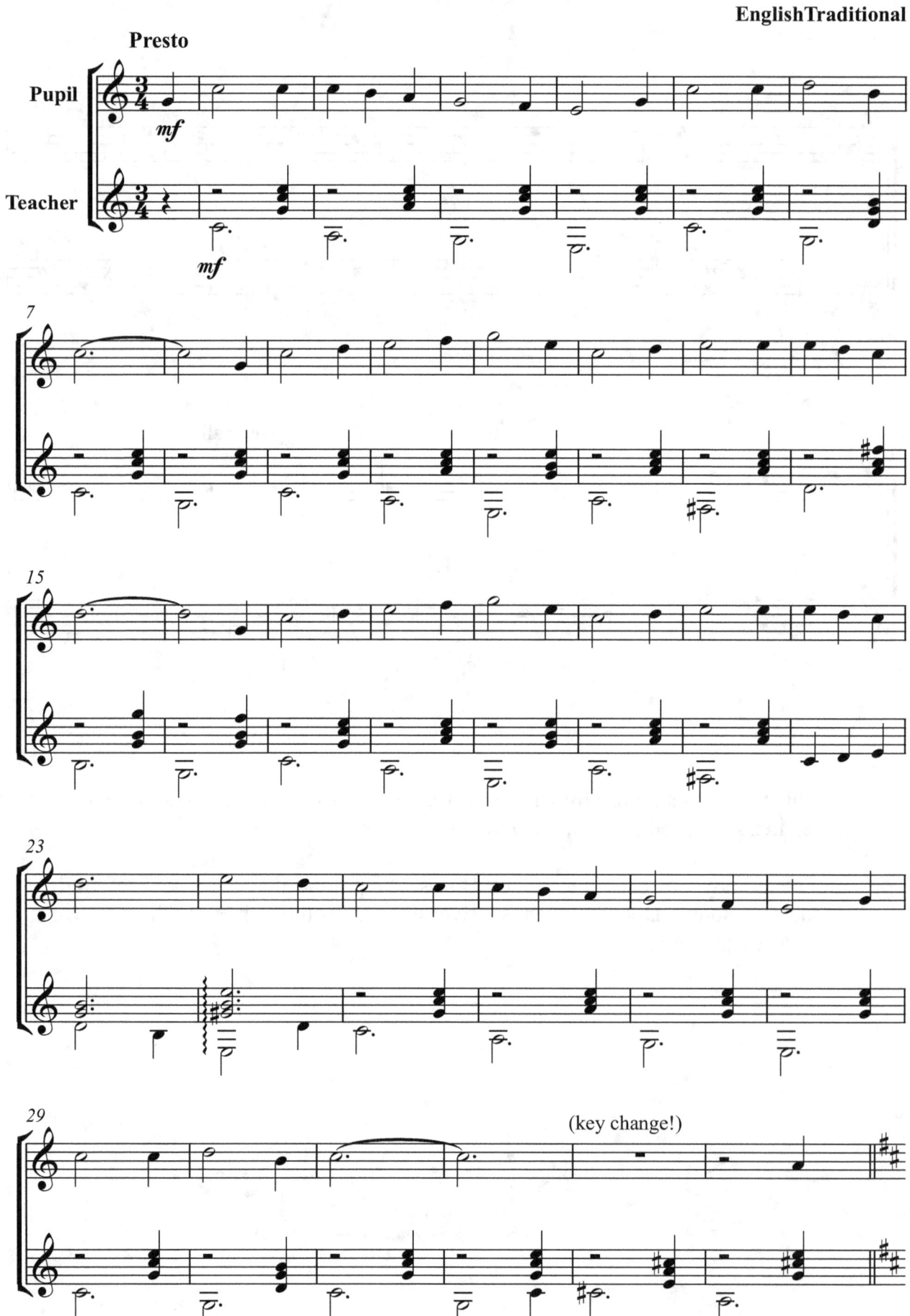

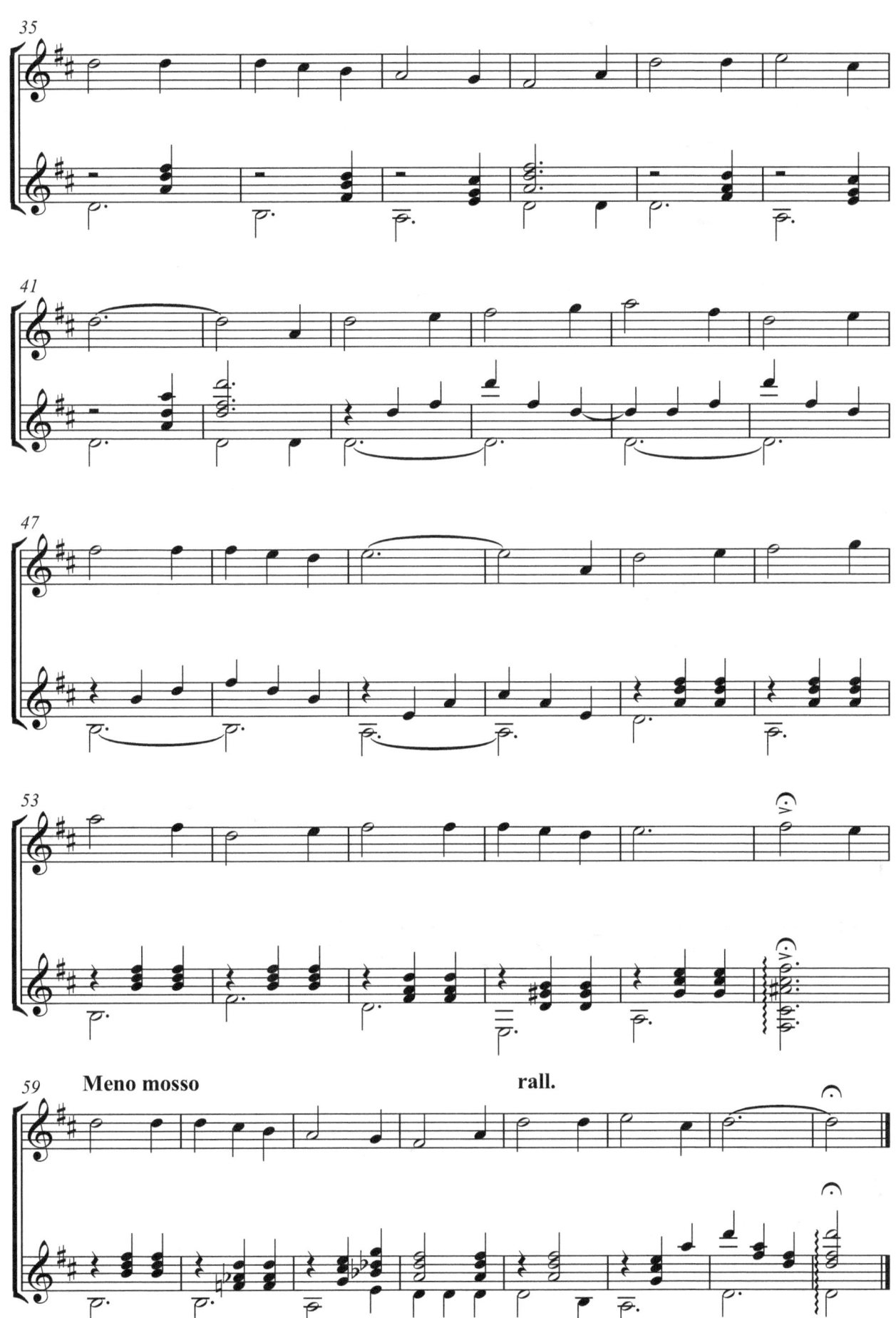

Bonny Mary of Argyle

Traditional

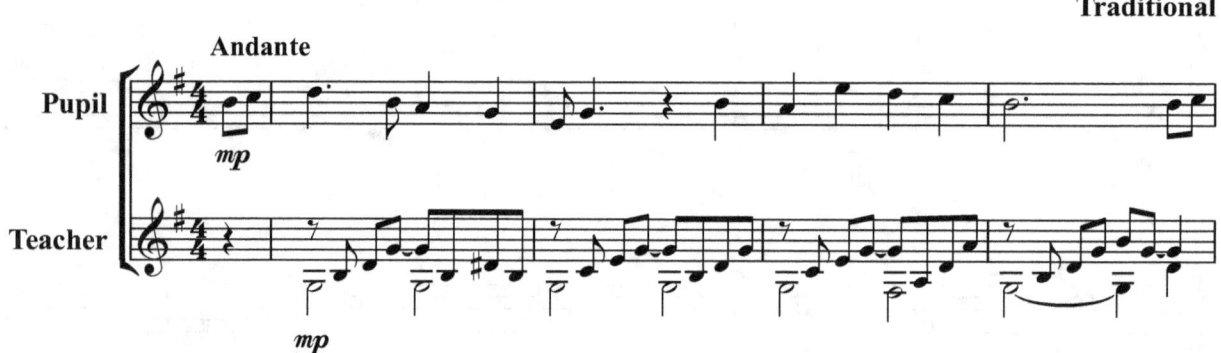

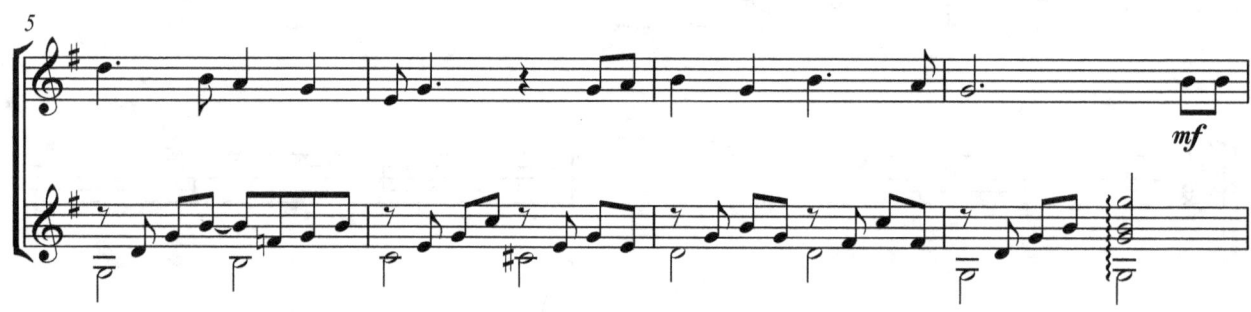

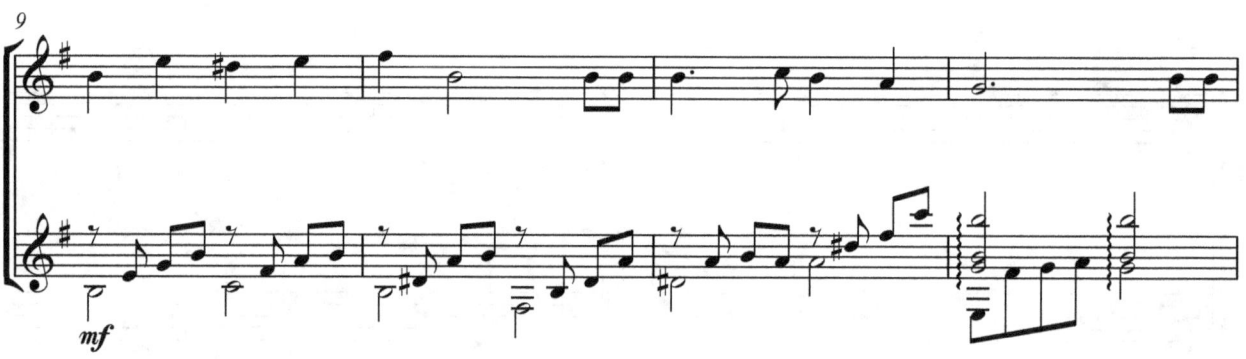

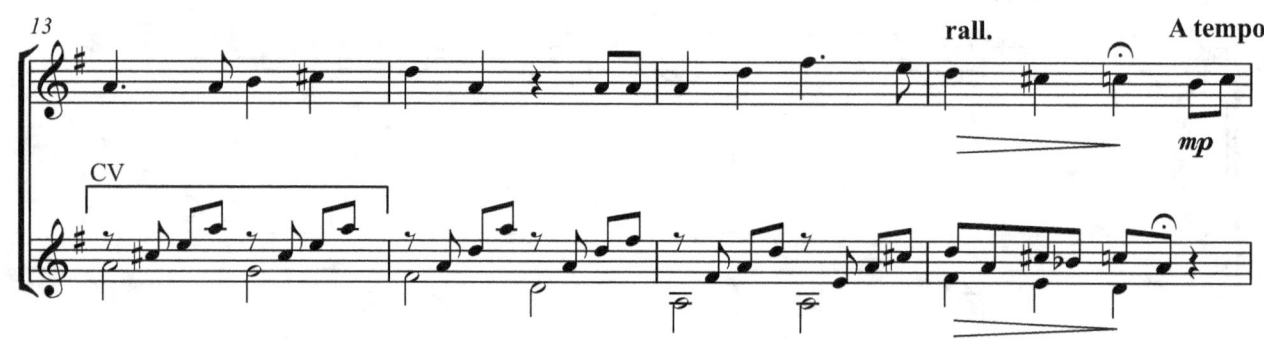

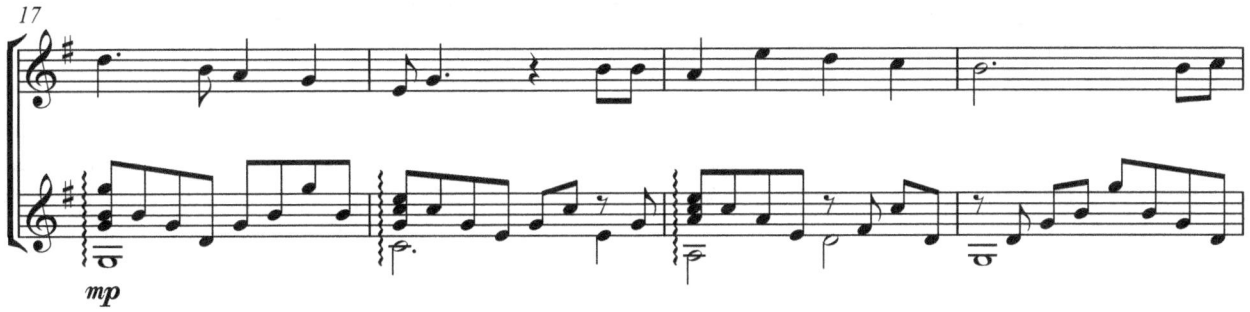

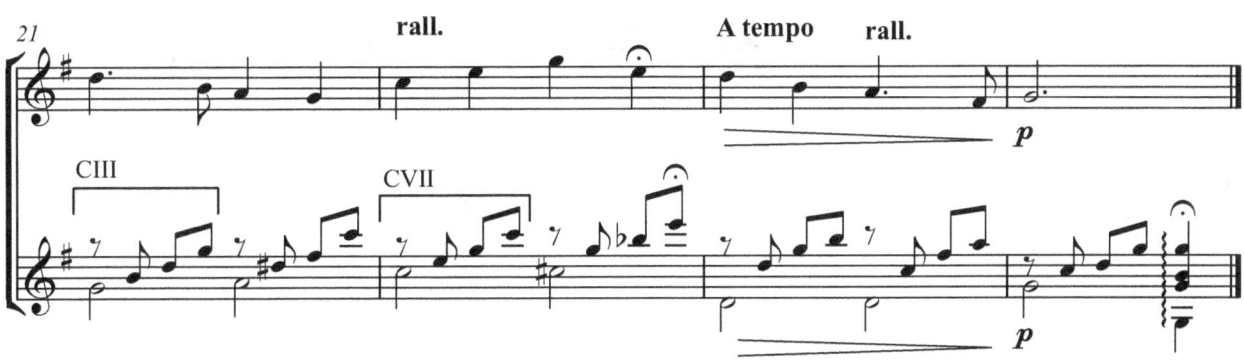

This piece is more harmonically and structurally ambitious than all the others in this book. It was composed around 1850, so is probably more of a "Victorian Ballad" than a folksong that has been passed on "by word of mouth".

The words describe Robert Burns' infatuation with Mary Campbell, otherwise known as "Highland Mary", who died at the very young age of 23. A statue of Mary overlooks the River Clyde in the town of Dunoon.

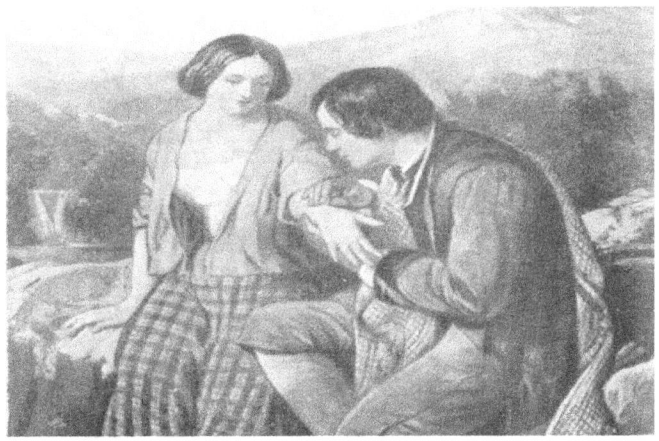

Cockles and Mussels

Old Dublin Street Song

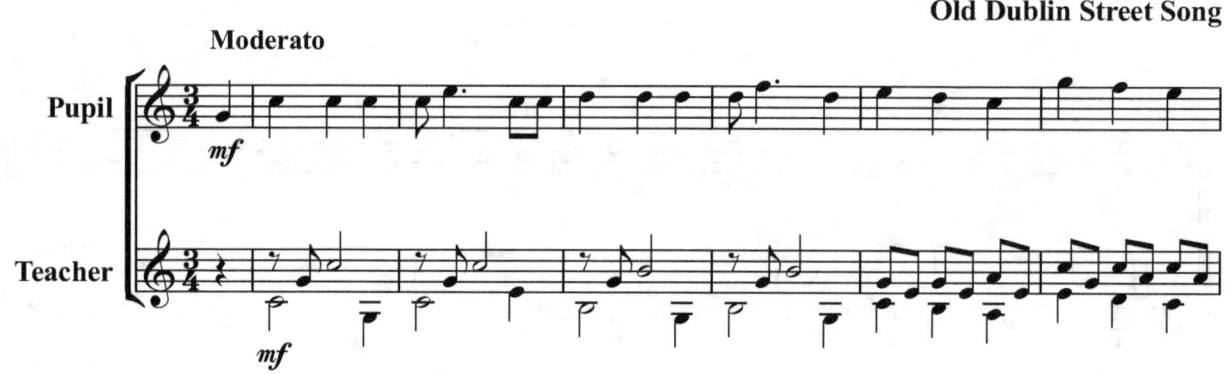

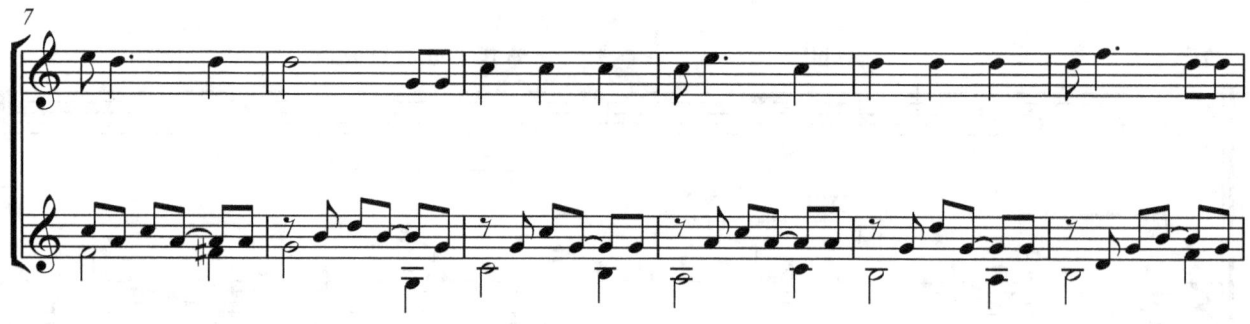

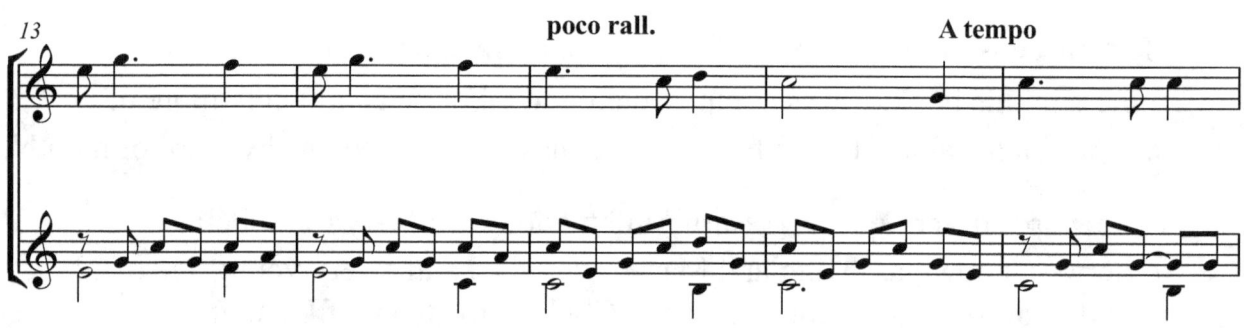

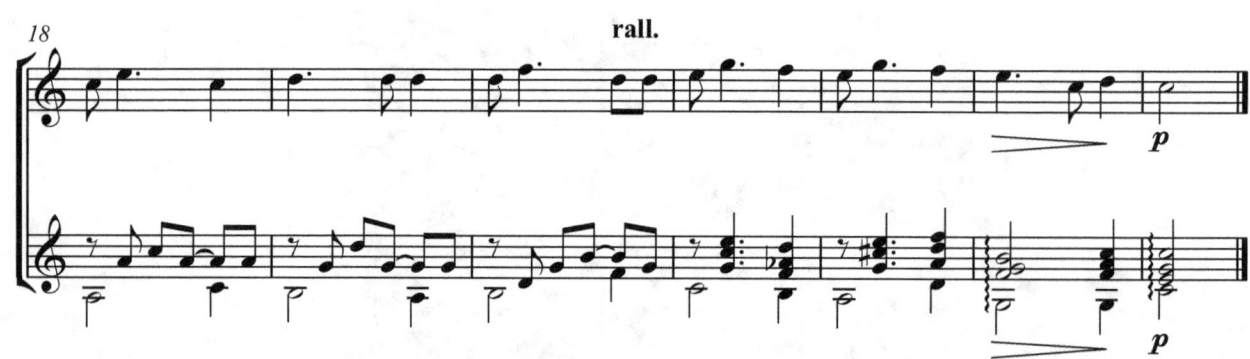

An Eriskay Love Lilt

Traditional

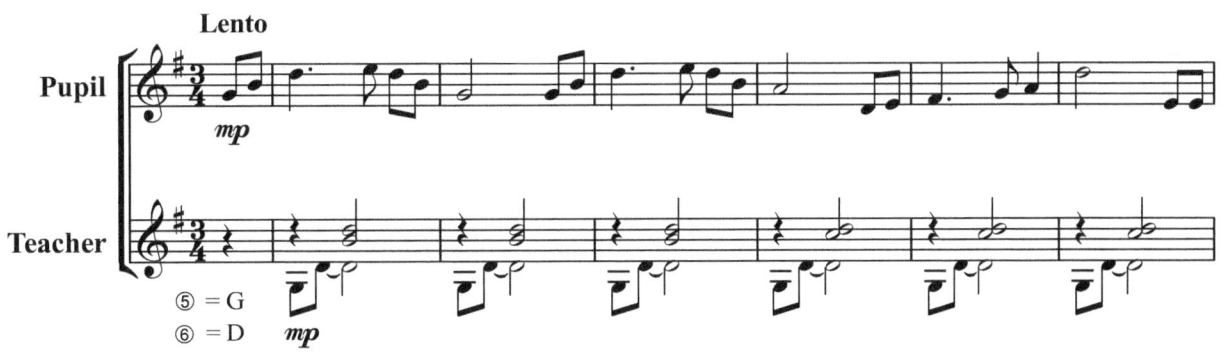

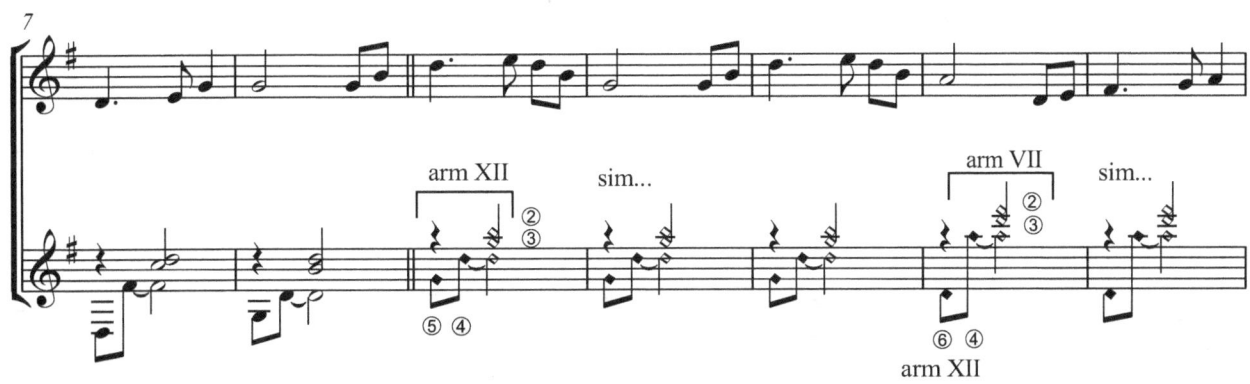

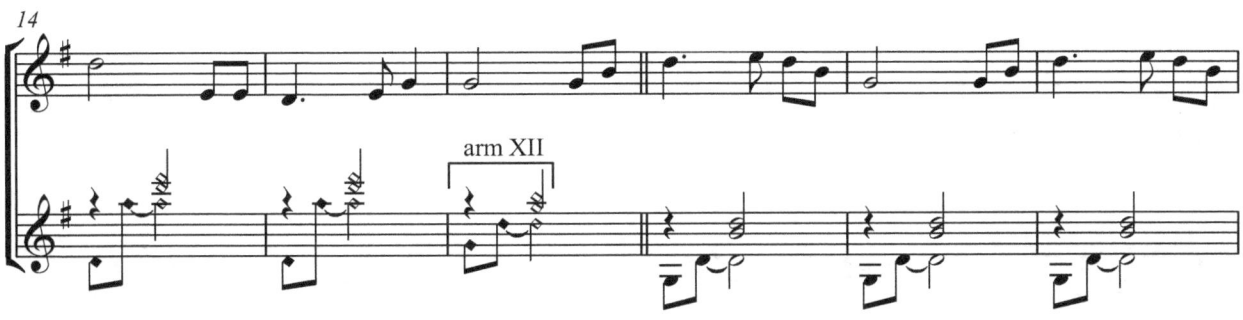

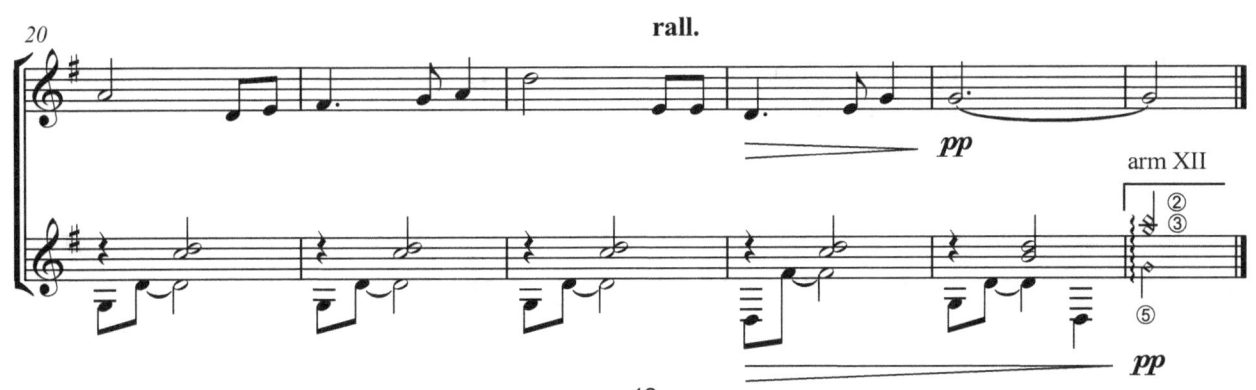

The Bluebells of Scotland

Attr. Dora Jordan

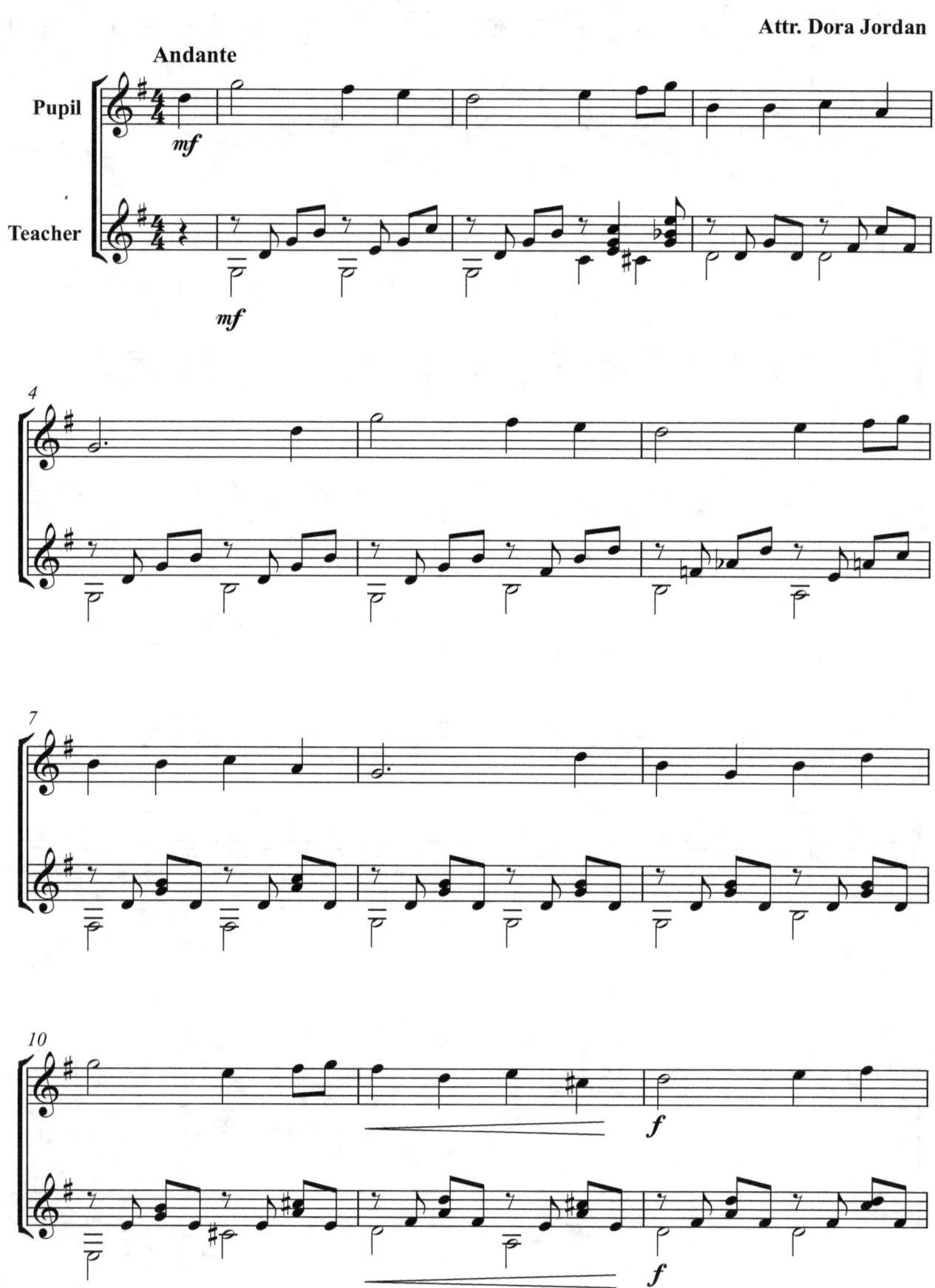

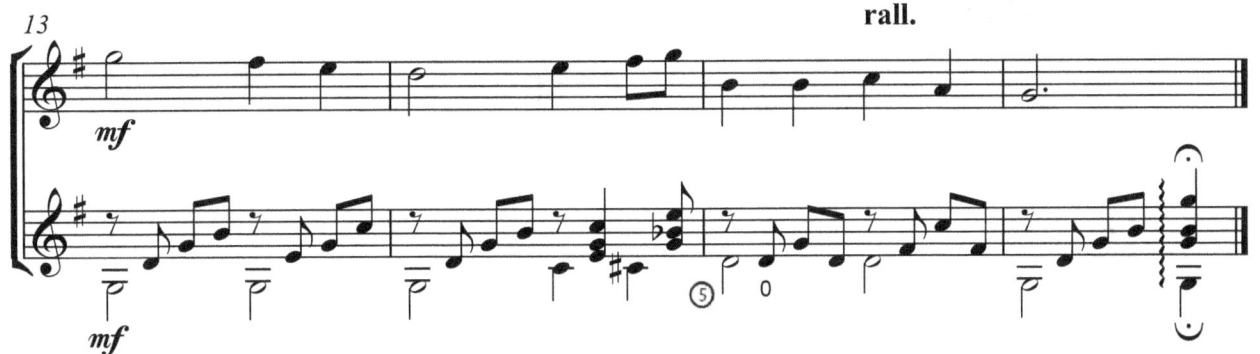

This popular song is supposed to have been written by Dora Jordan,
a famous London actress. It was first published in 1801.

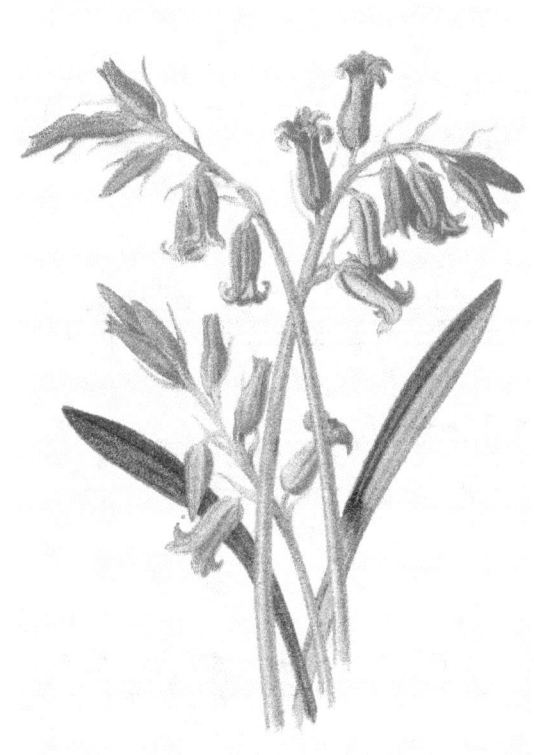

Men of Harlech

Welsh Traditional

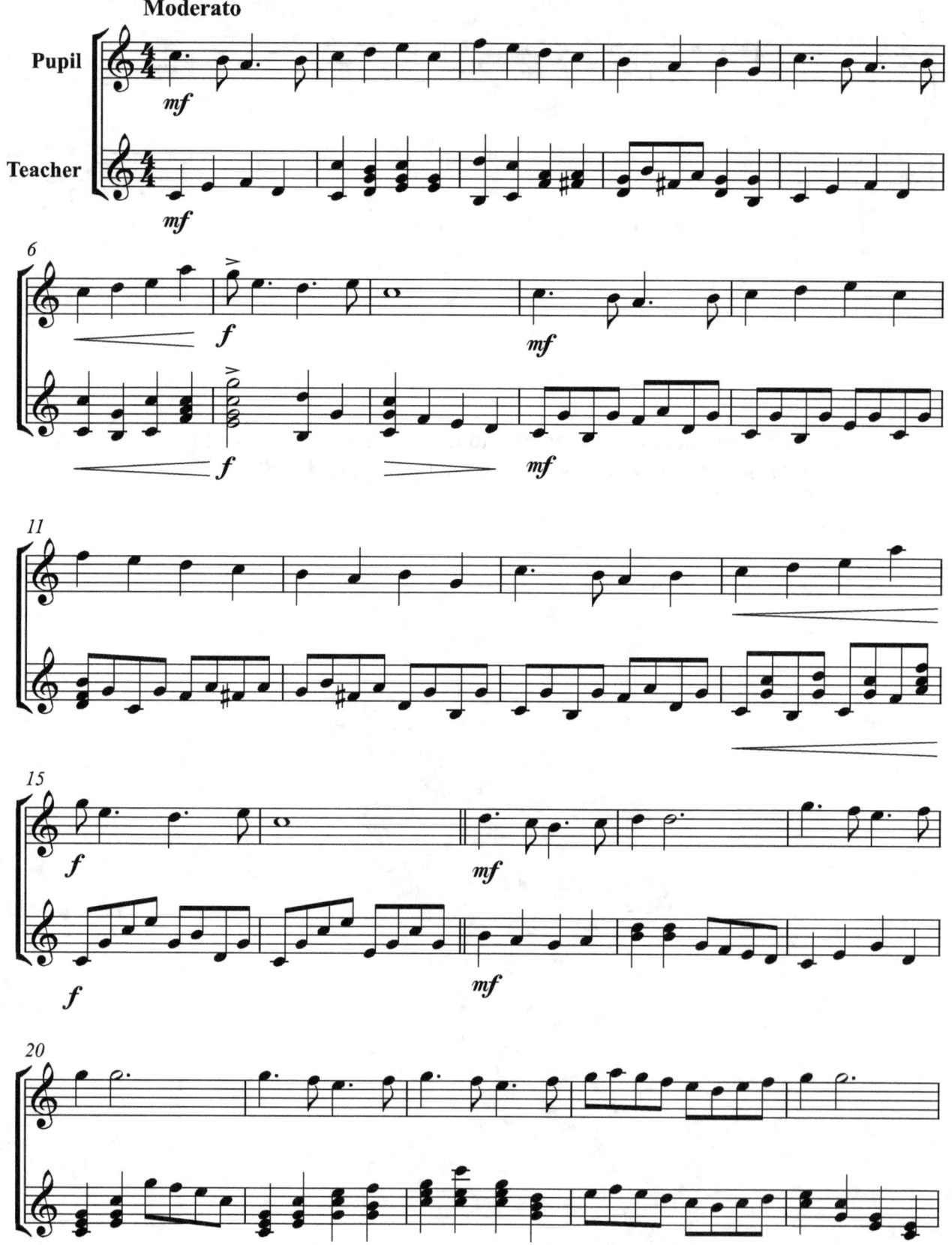

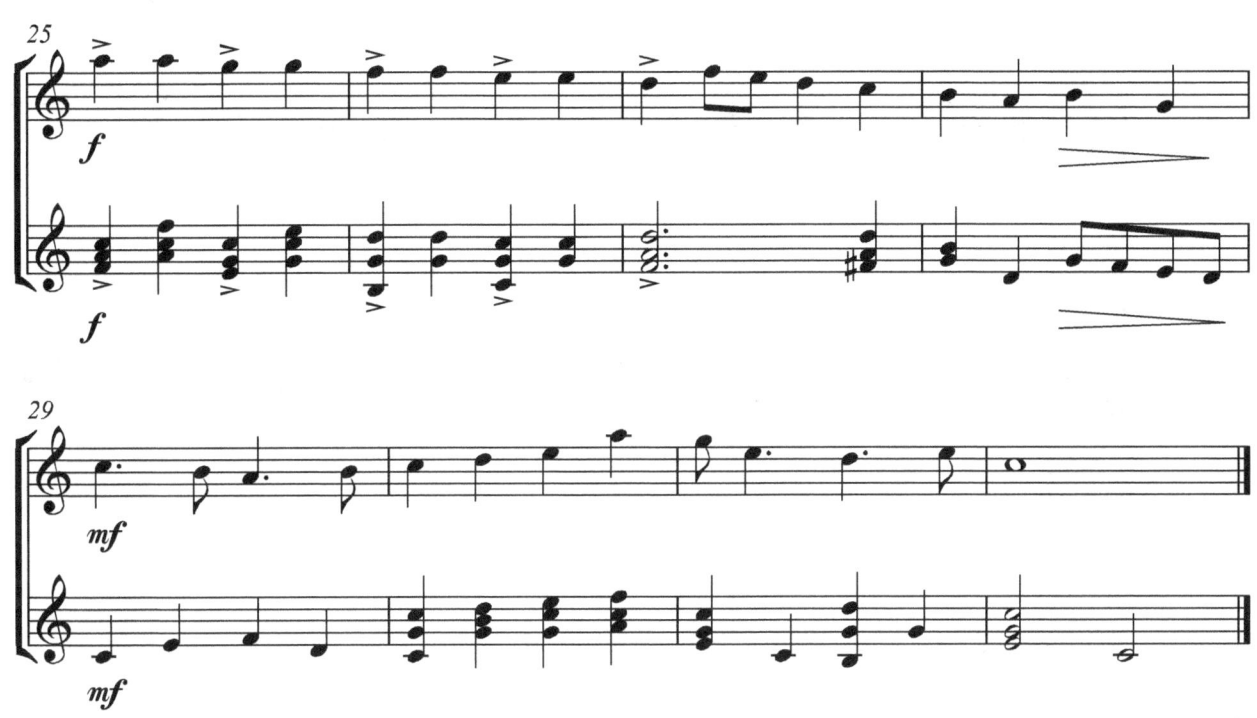

It has been said that this famous march, often mistaken as the Welsh national anthem, was composed during the War of the Roses, when Harlech Castle was besieged on behalf of Edward IV in 1468.

The siege lasted for seven years. After the garrison surrendered, all of England and Wales came under Yorkist control.

My Love Is Like a Red, Red Rose

Traditional

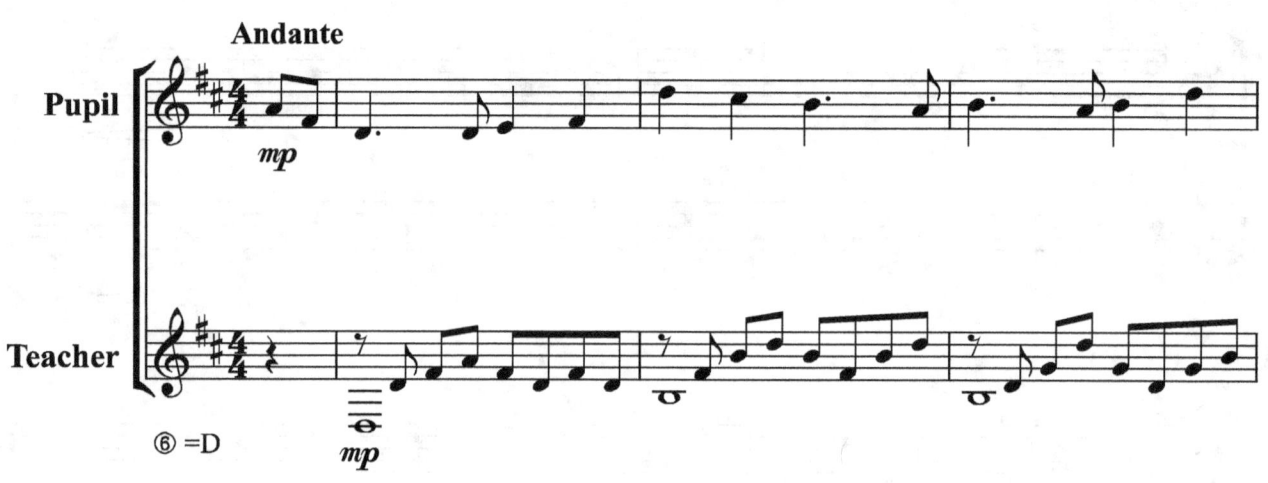

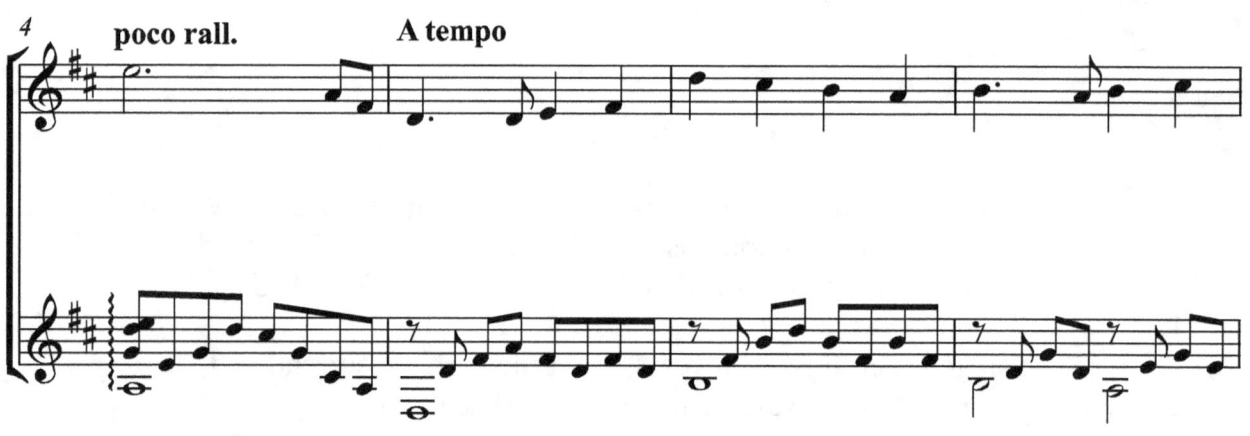

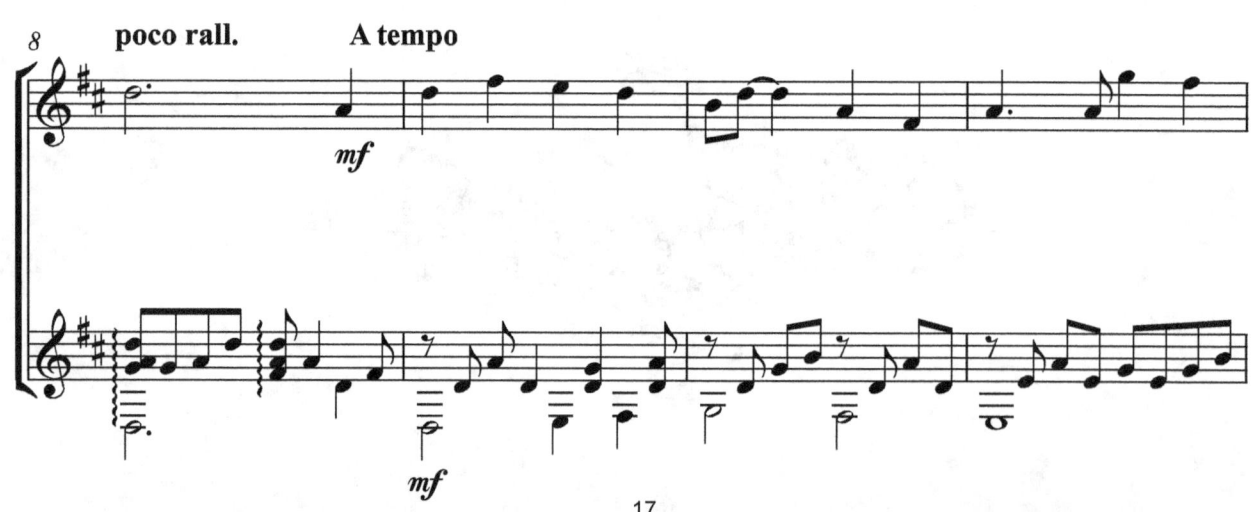

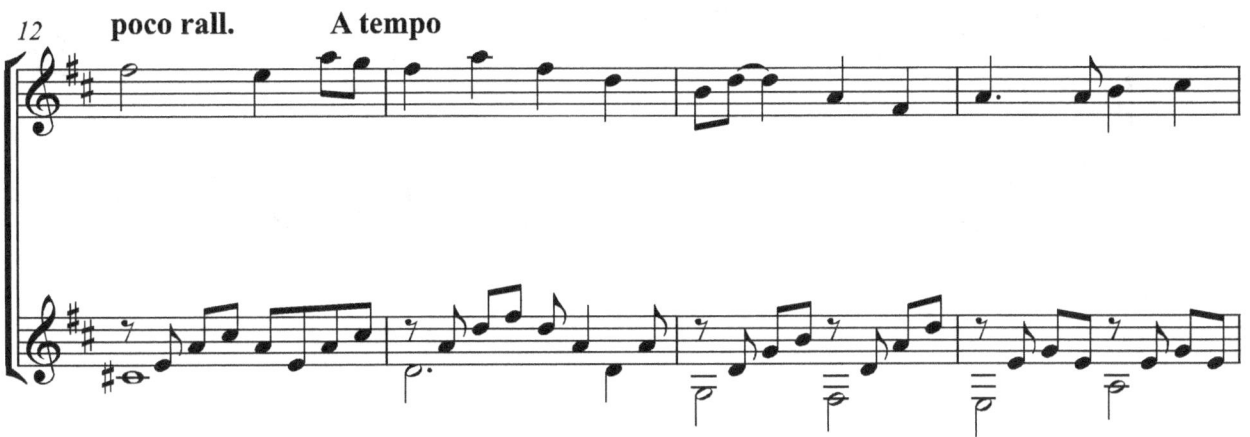

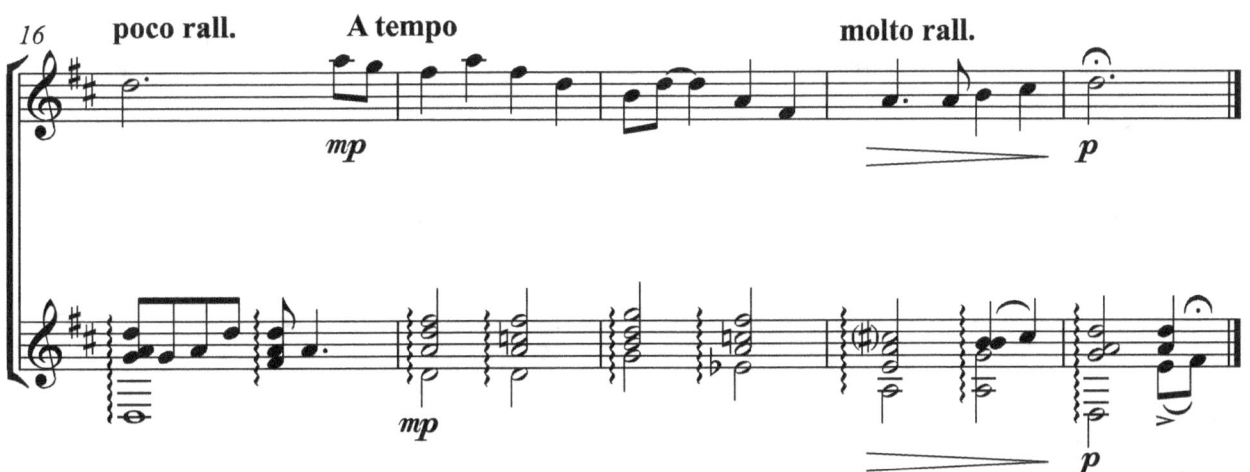

In the final years of Burns' life, he set out to preserve for posterity a body of Scottish songs.
This song was not written from scratch by Burns, but based on traditional sources.
When it was first published in 1797 it was paired with a melody known as "Major Graham"
by Neil Gow, which was the choice of Burns.
It was not until 1821 that the song was given its now familiar melody.

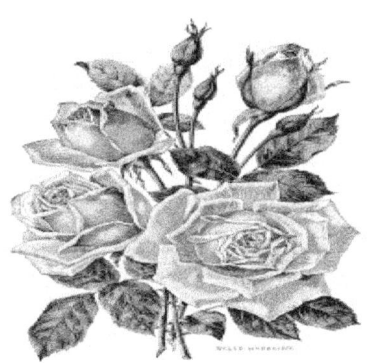

On The Banks of Cairnie Burn

Adrian Allan

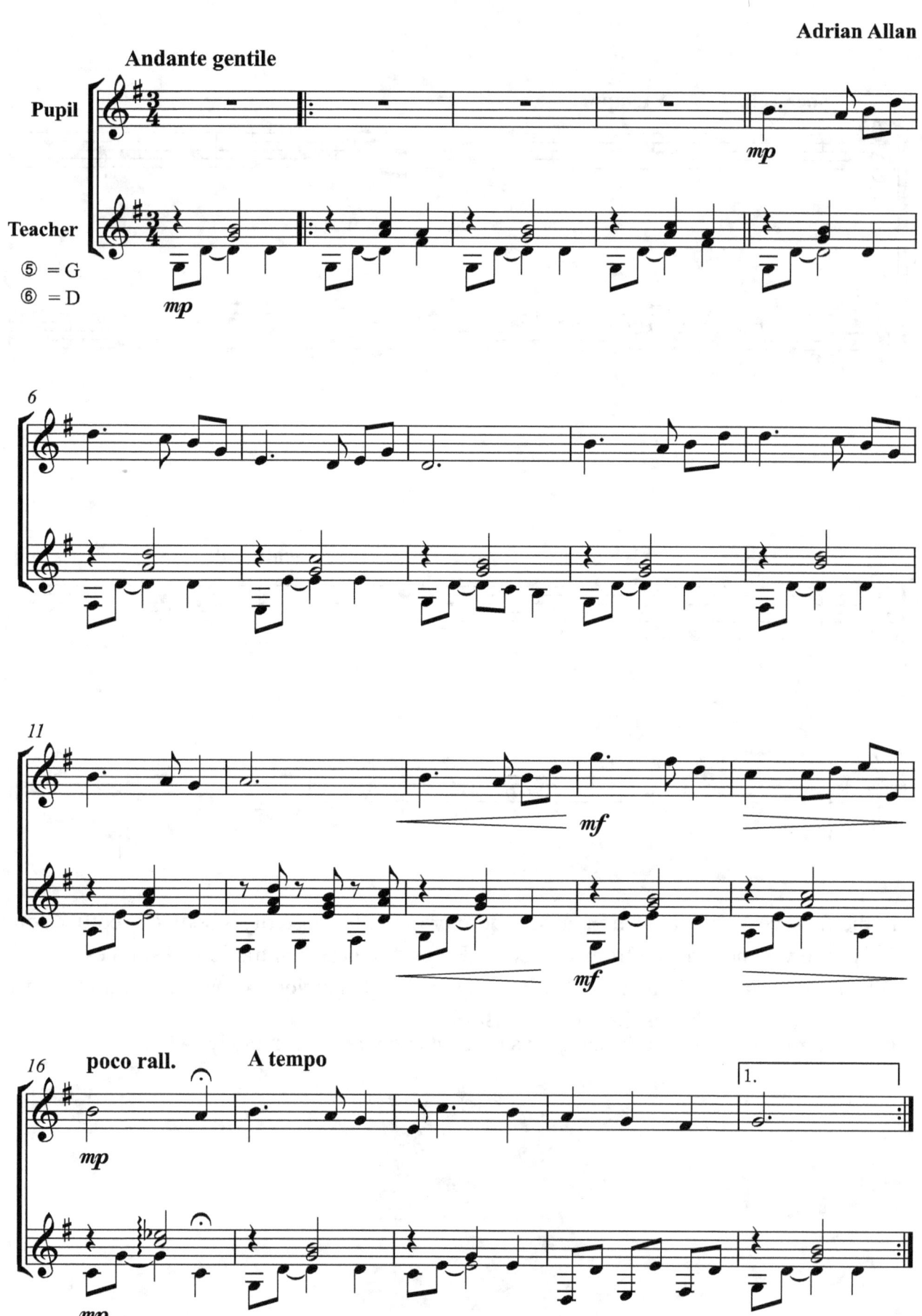

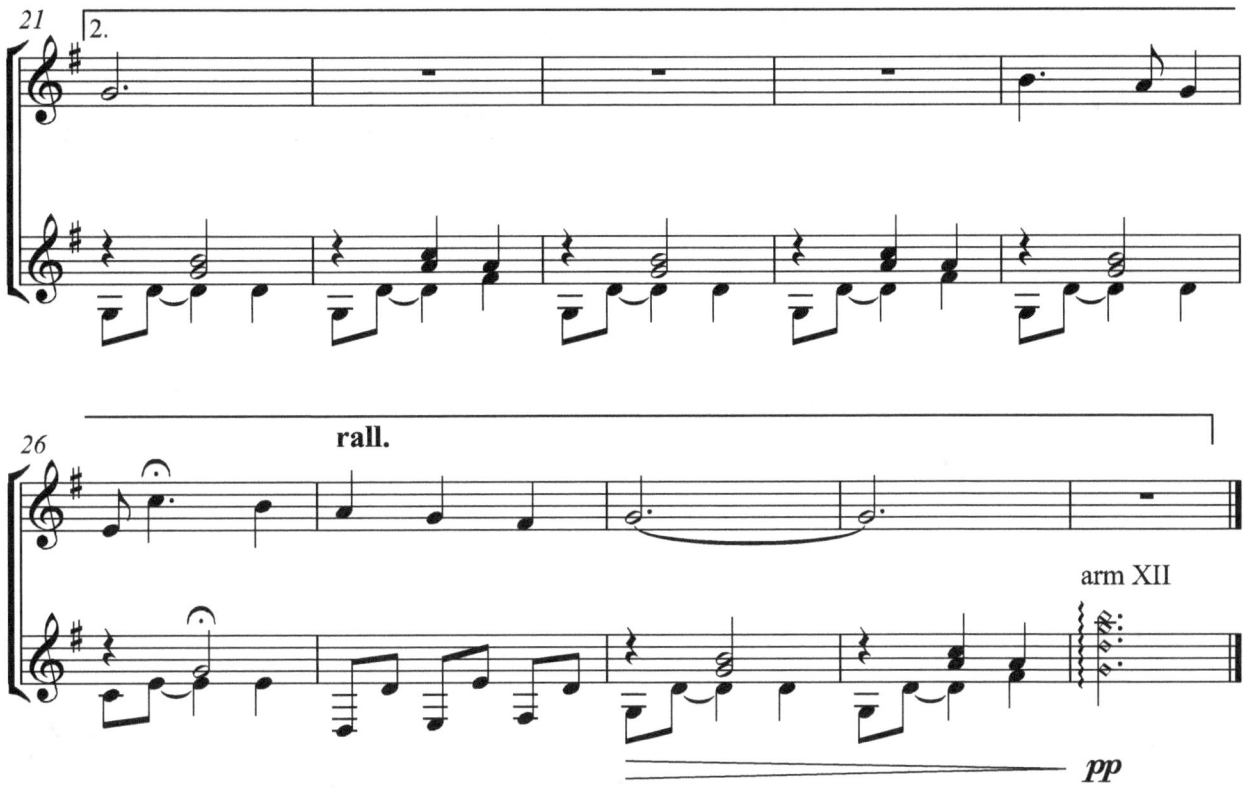

This is the only original piece in this book. I set myself the challenge of writing
a piece in the style of an old Scottish Air. I hope that I have captured some of that spirit.

Performance note:

The teacher part uses a G-tuning, with strings 6 and 5 dropped to D and G, respectively.
Please allow the strings to freely vibrate. This accompaniment should be rich and
resonant. Folk musicians don't tend to worry about over-ringing harmonies.

The Oak and the Ash

English Traditional

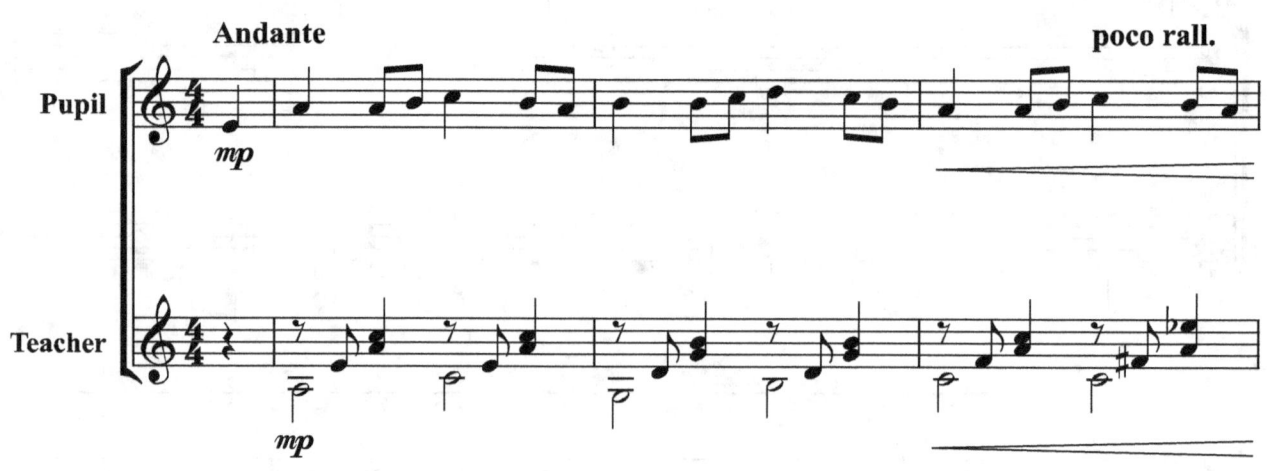

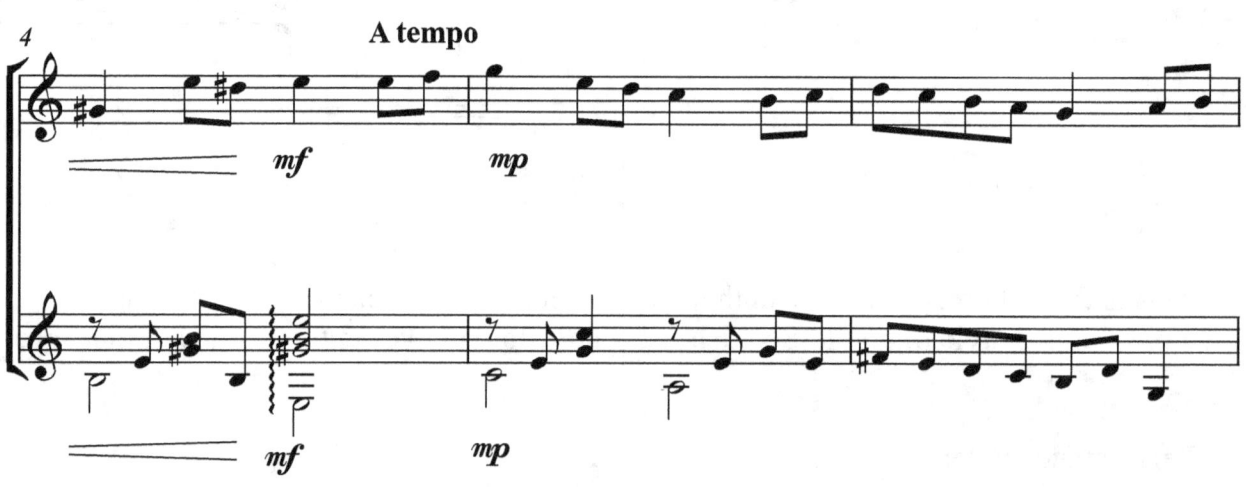

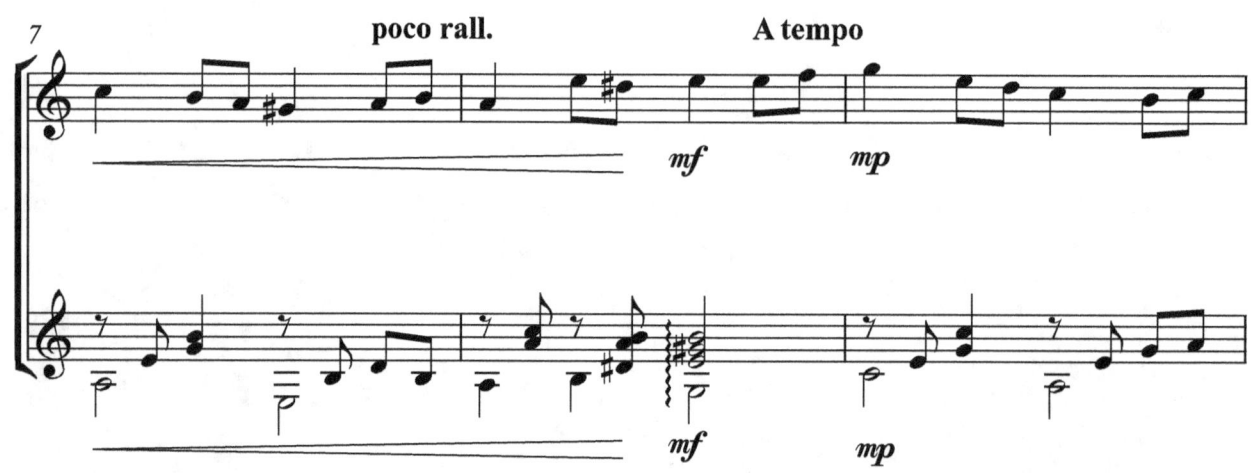

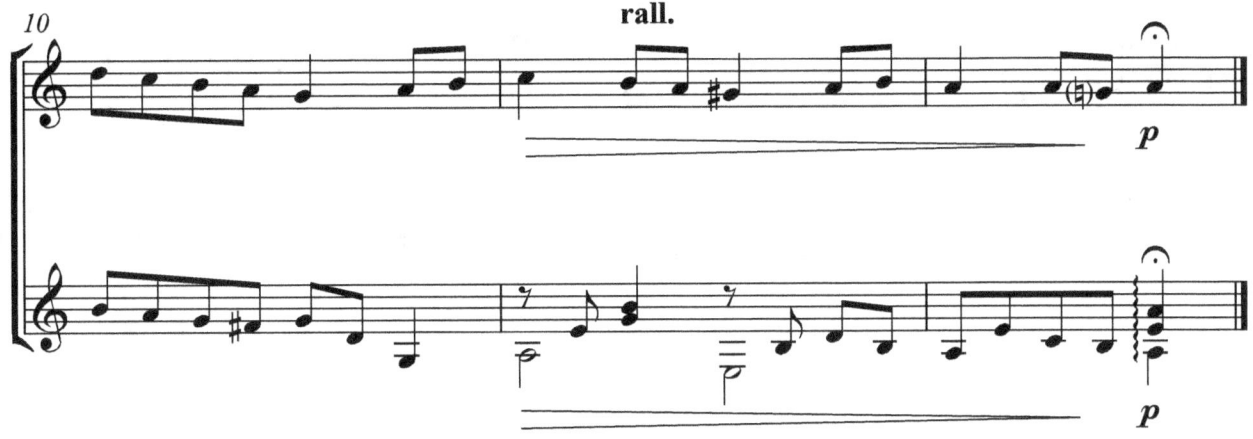

This is a very old melody, dating back to the early 1600's. It appears in the Fitzwilliam Virginal Book.

The lyrics concern the homesickness of a "north country maid", who has moved to London. She laments, that the Oak and the Ash tree, "flourish at home in my own country".

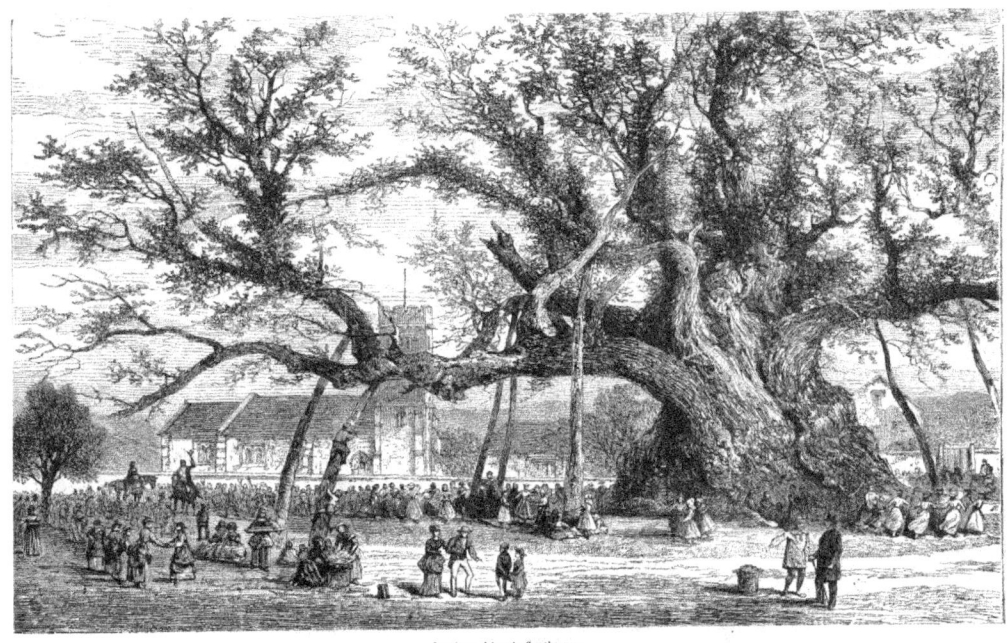

Le vieux chêne de Cowthorpe.

Allan Water

Monk Lewis

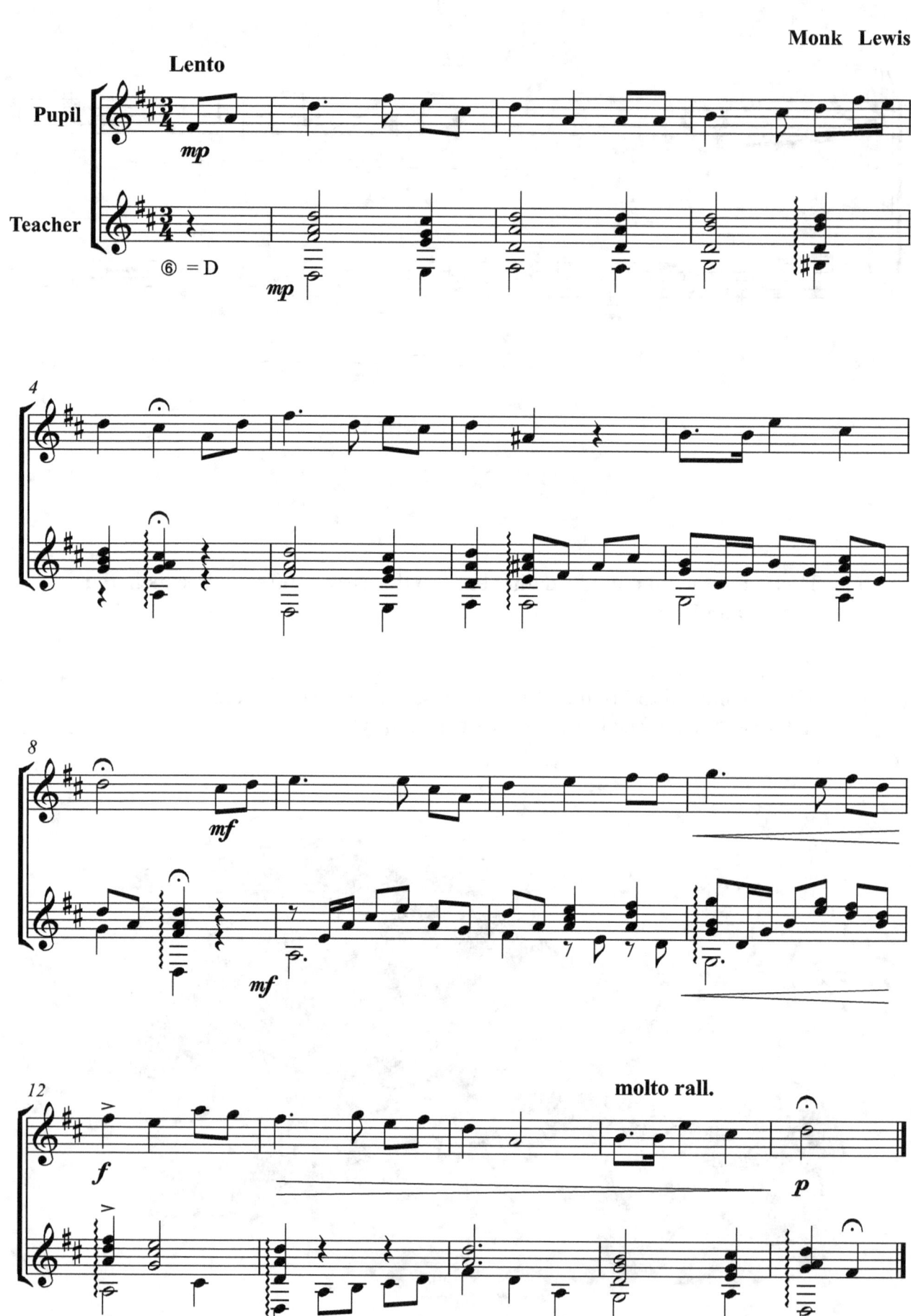

The Boar's Head Carol

Traditional

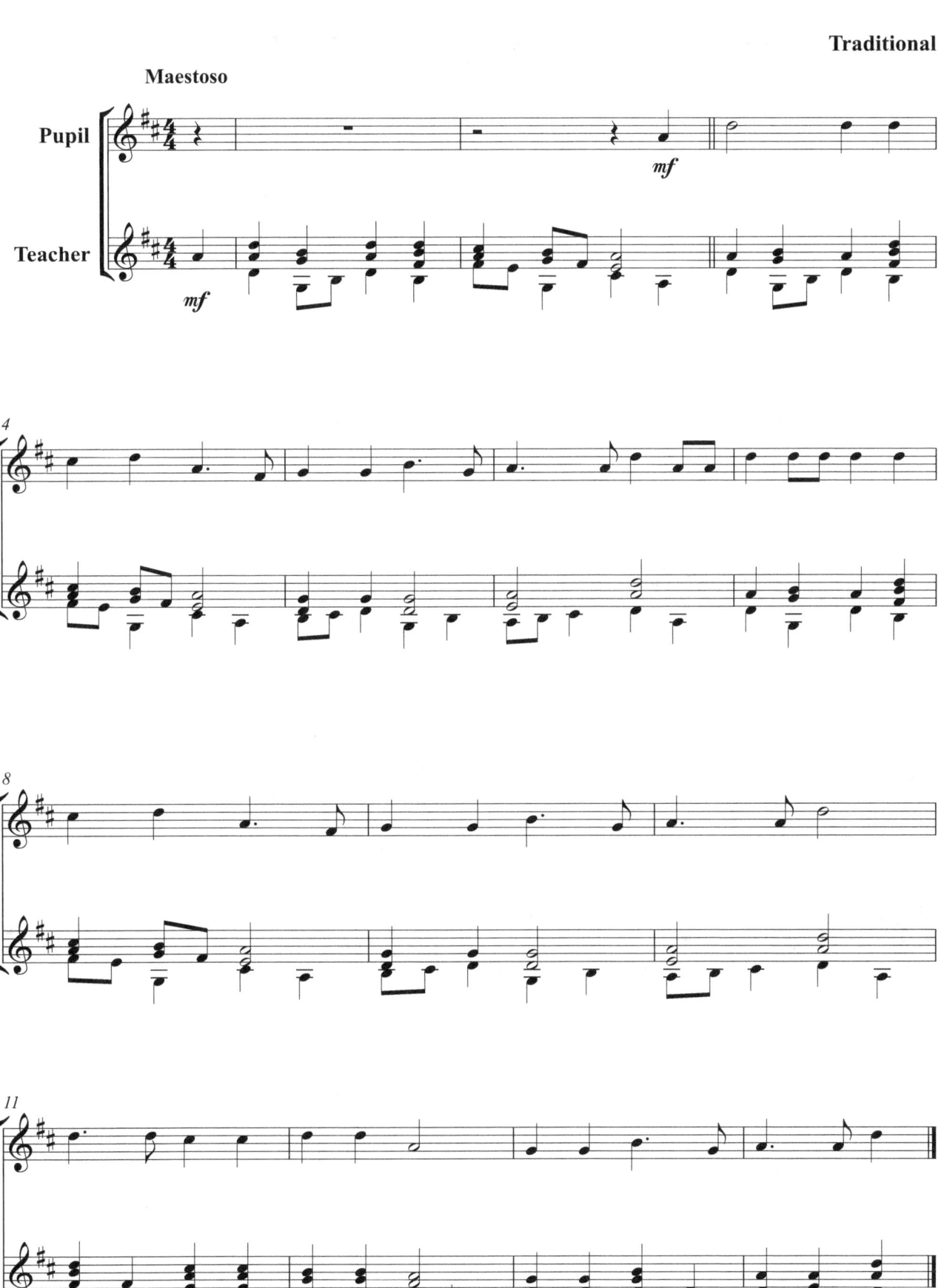

Land of My Fathers

James James

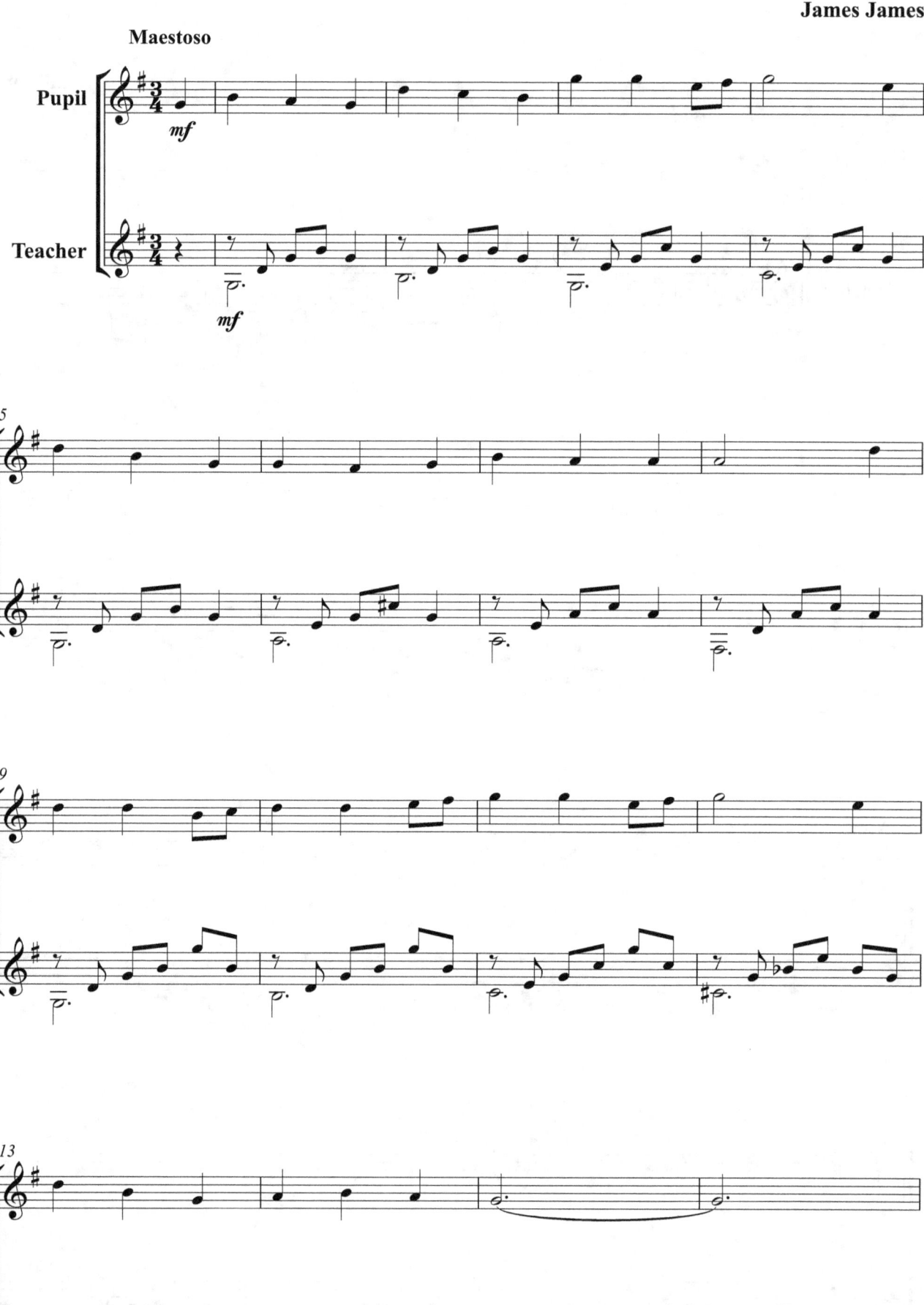

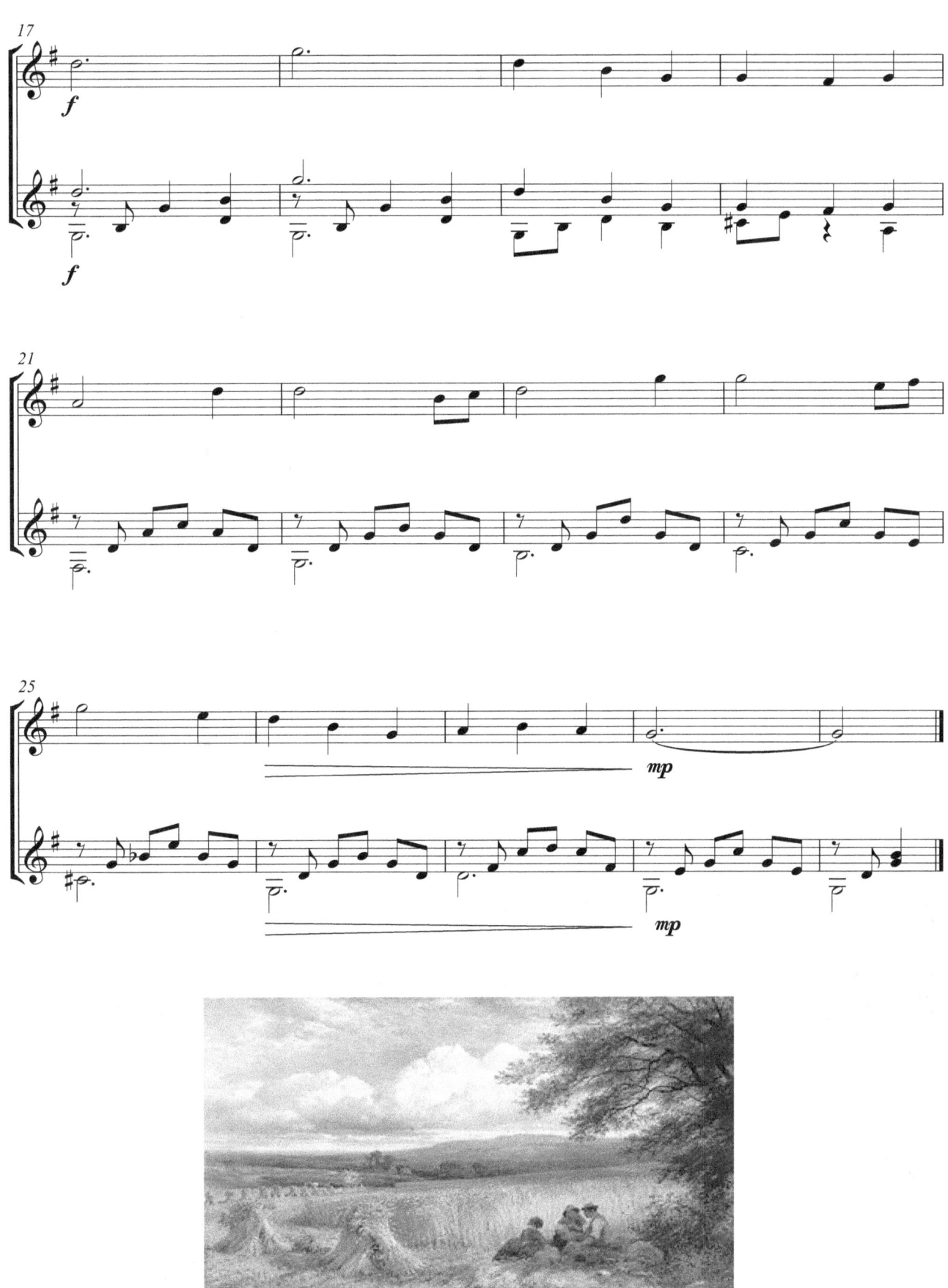

Drink To Me Only

Ben Jonson

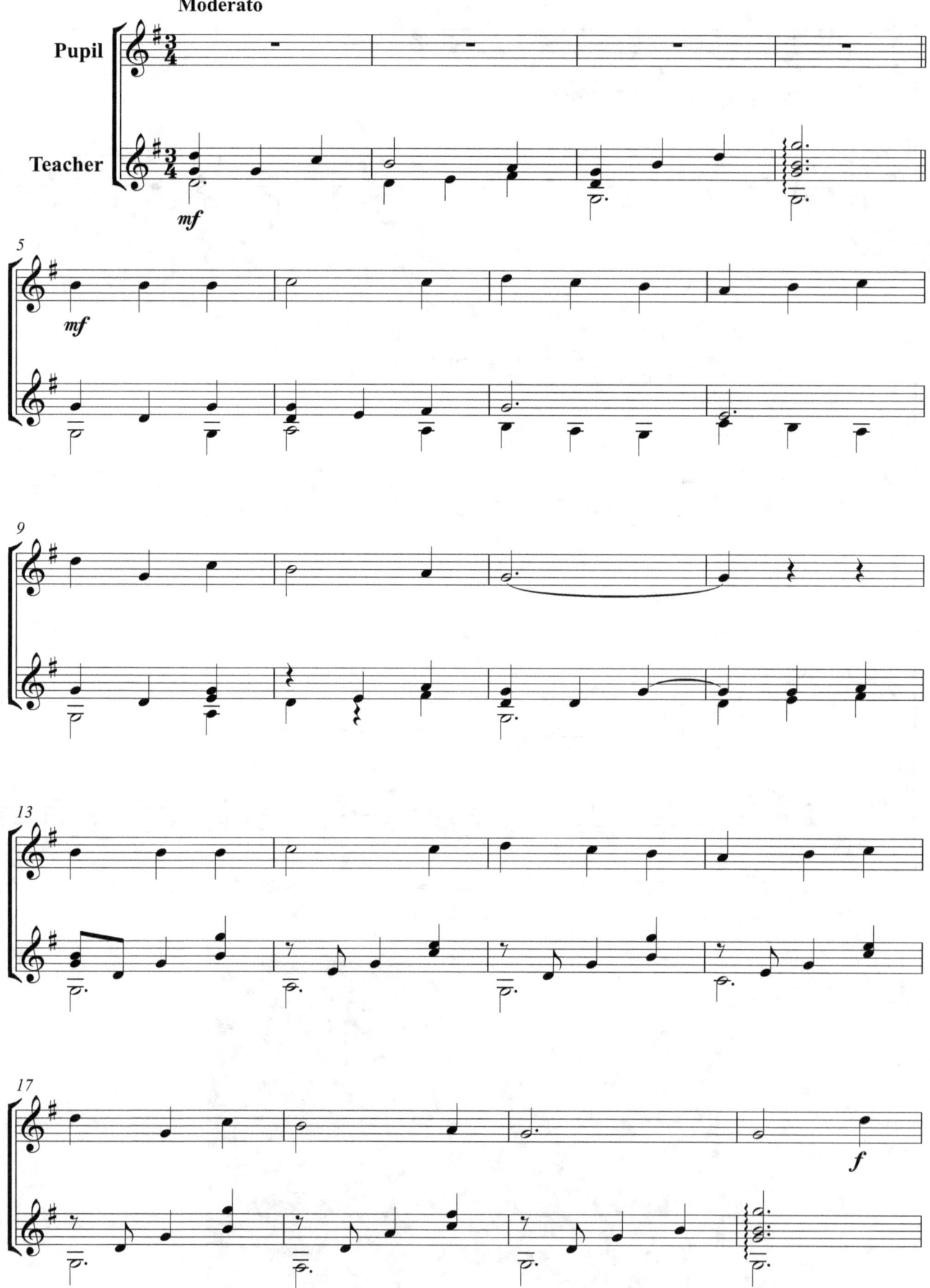

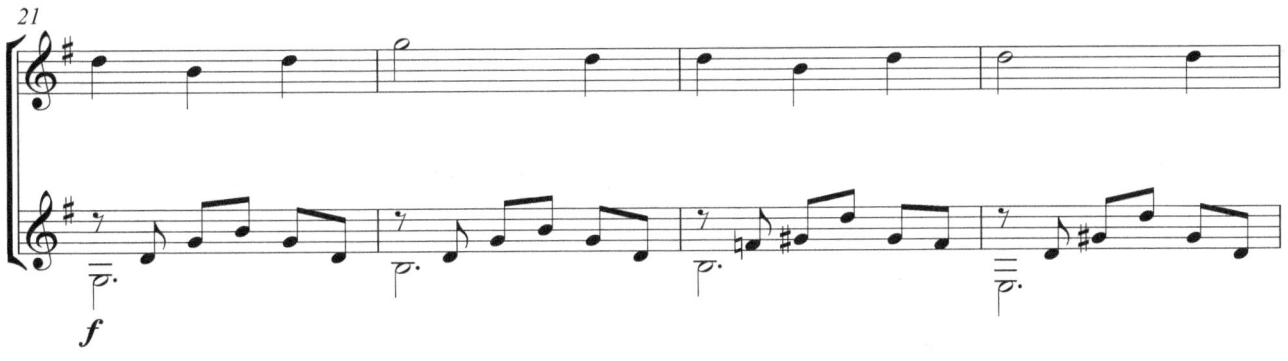

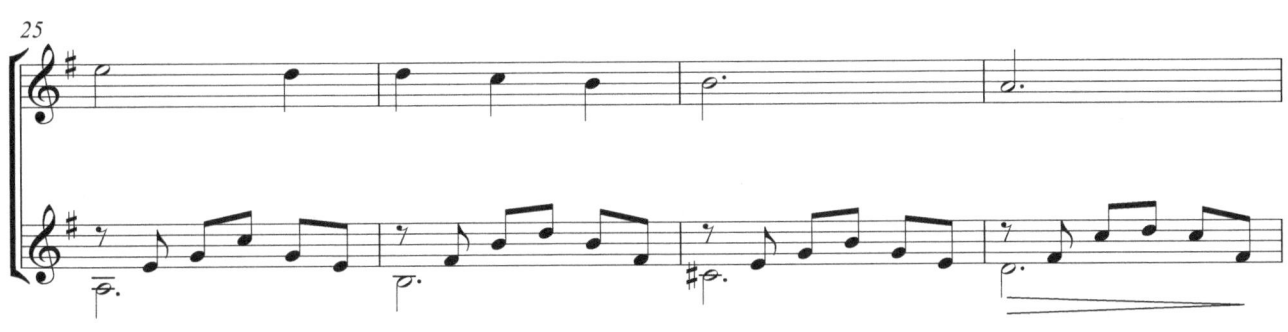

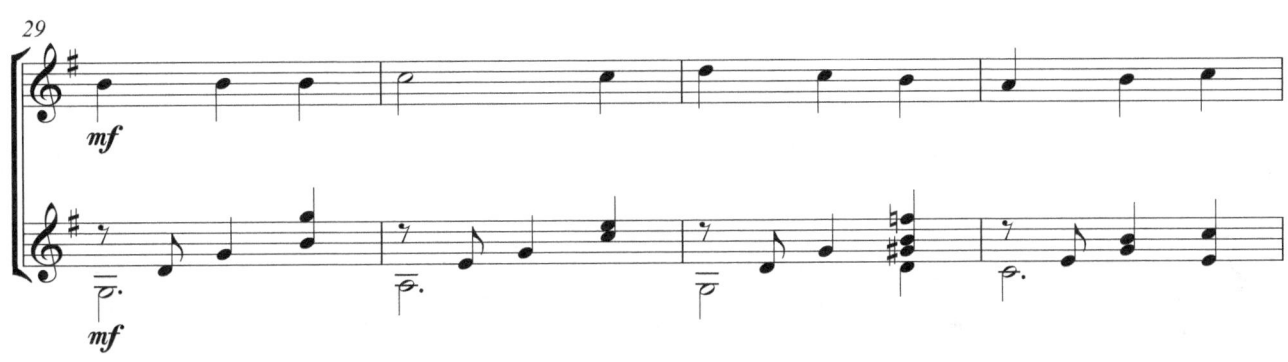

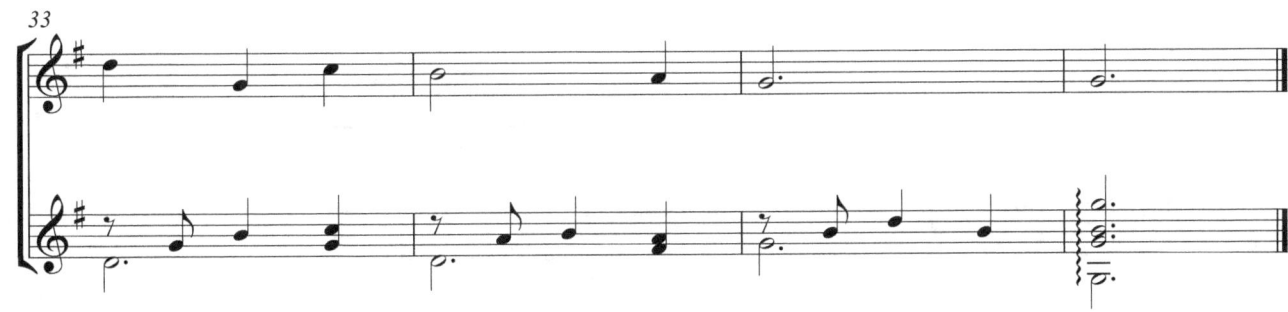

The Leaving of Liverpool

Traditional

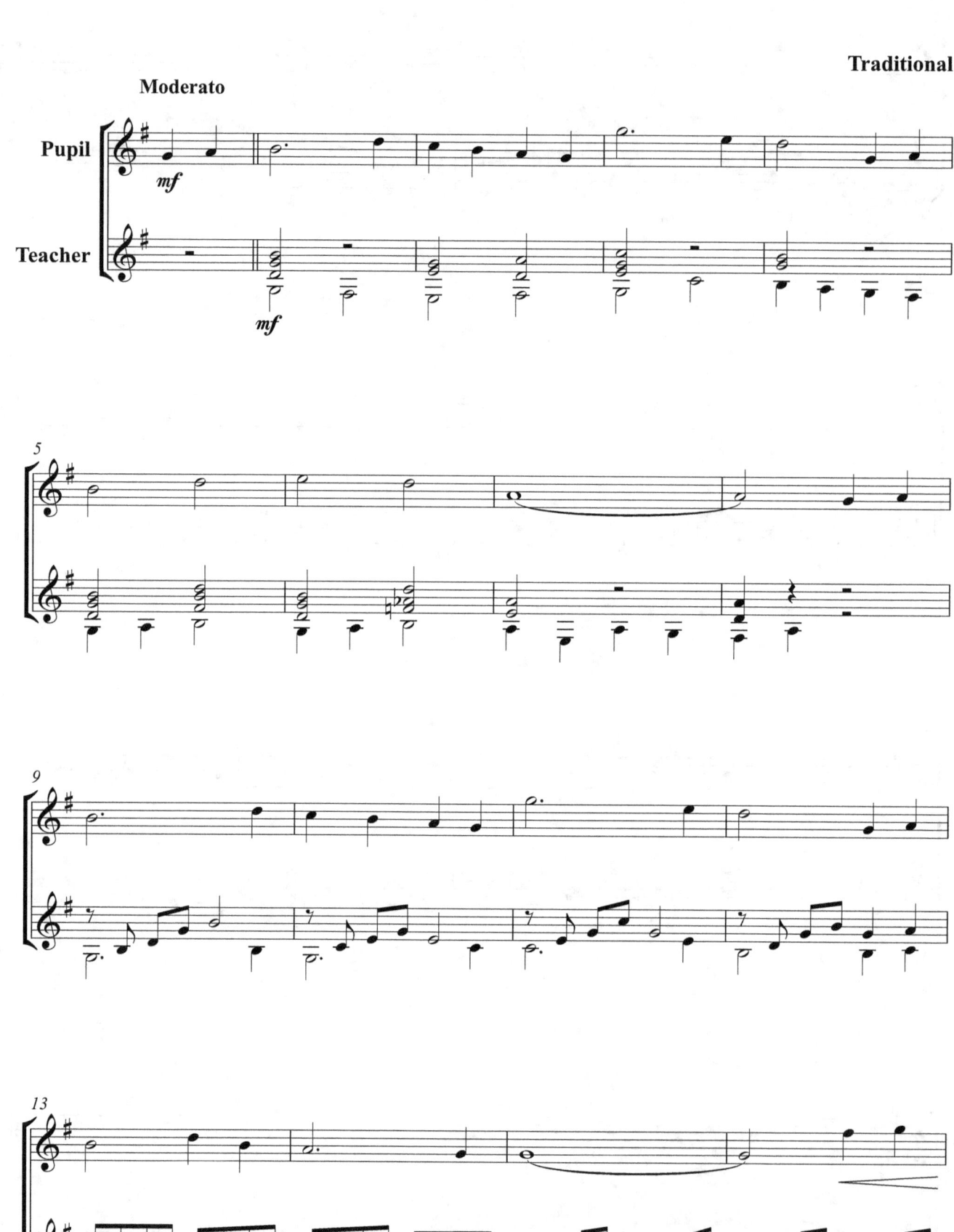

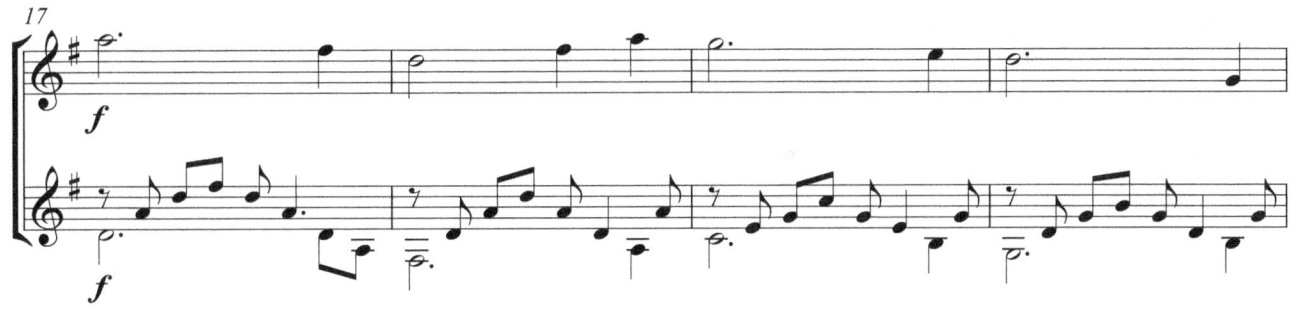

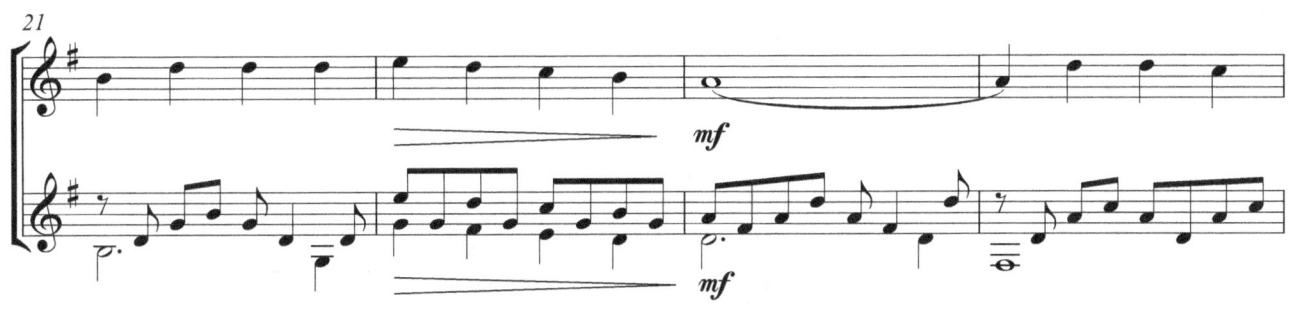

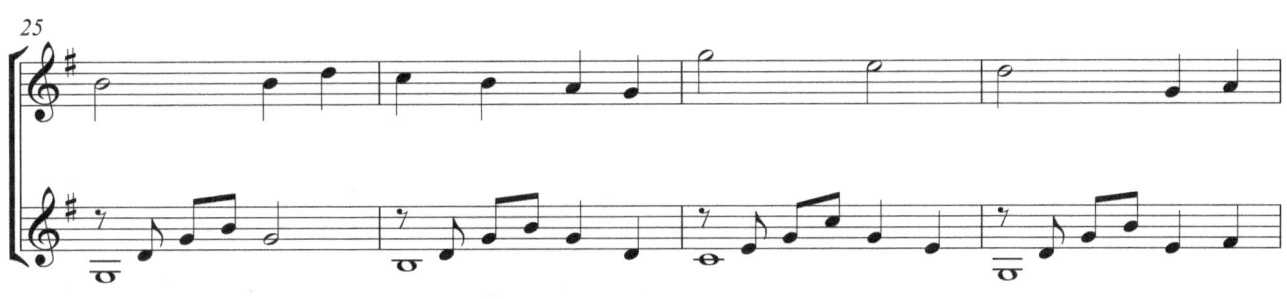

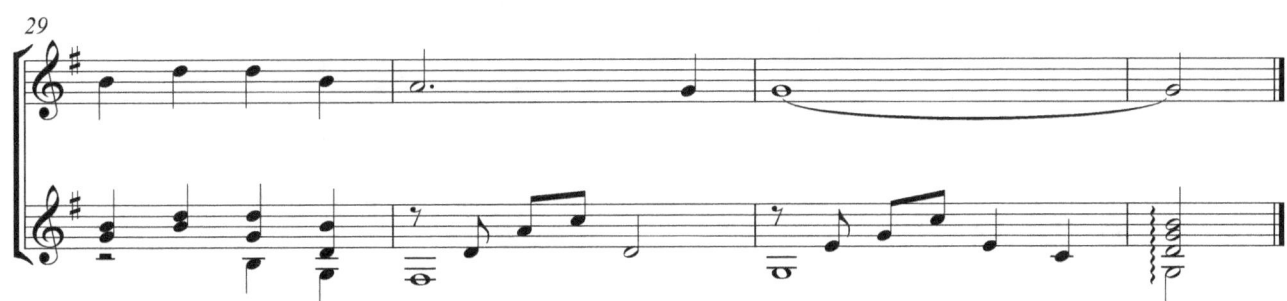

Henry Martin

Traditional

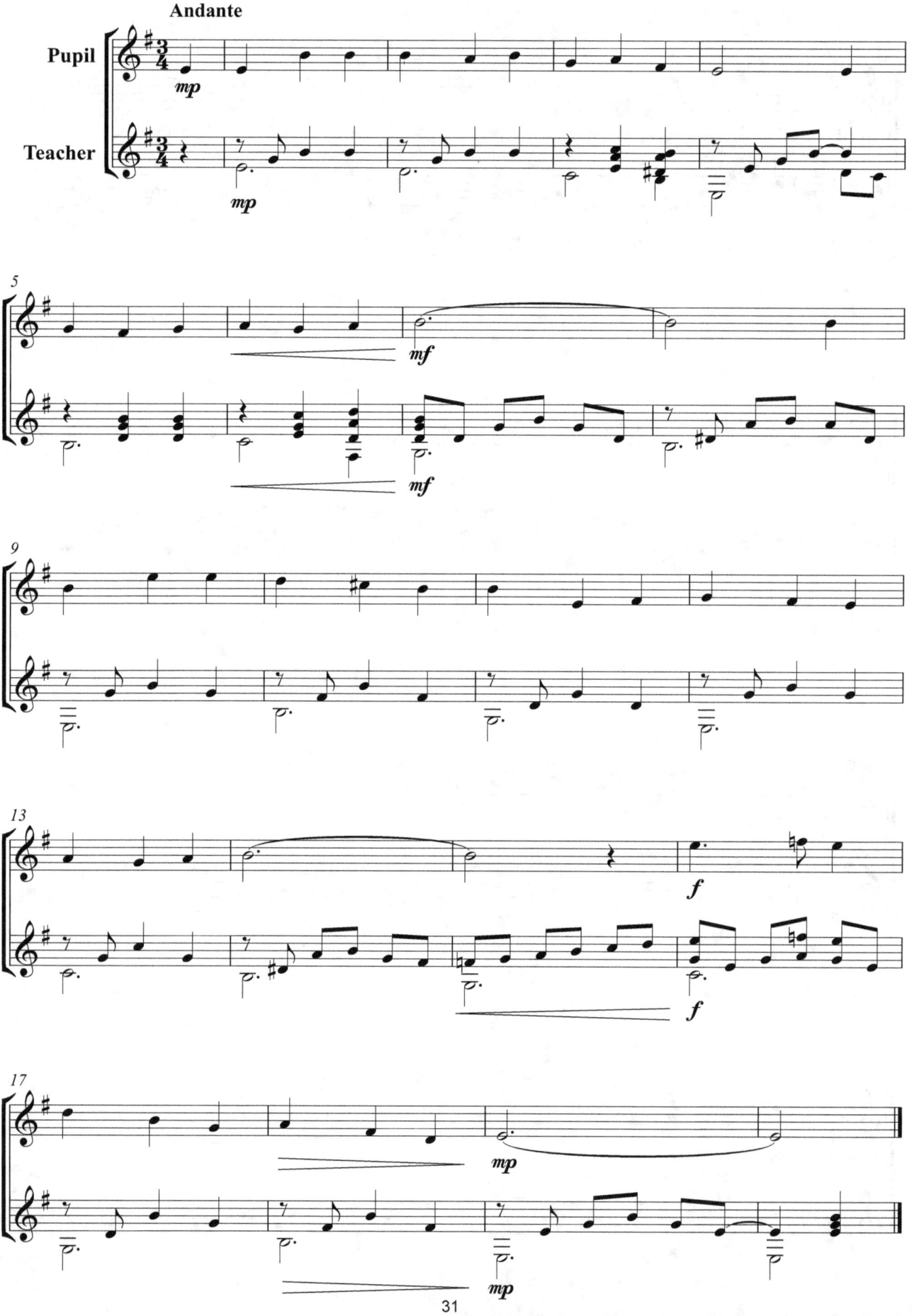

Annie Laurie

Traditional

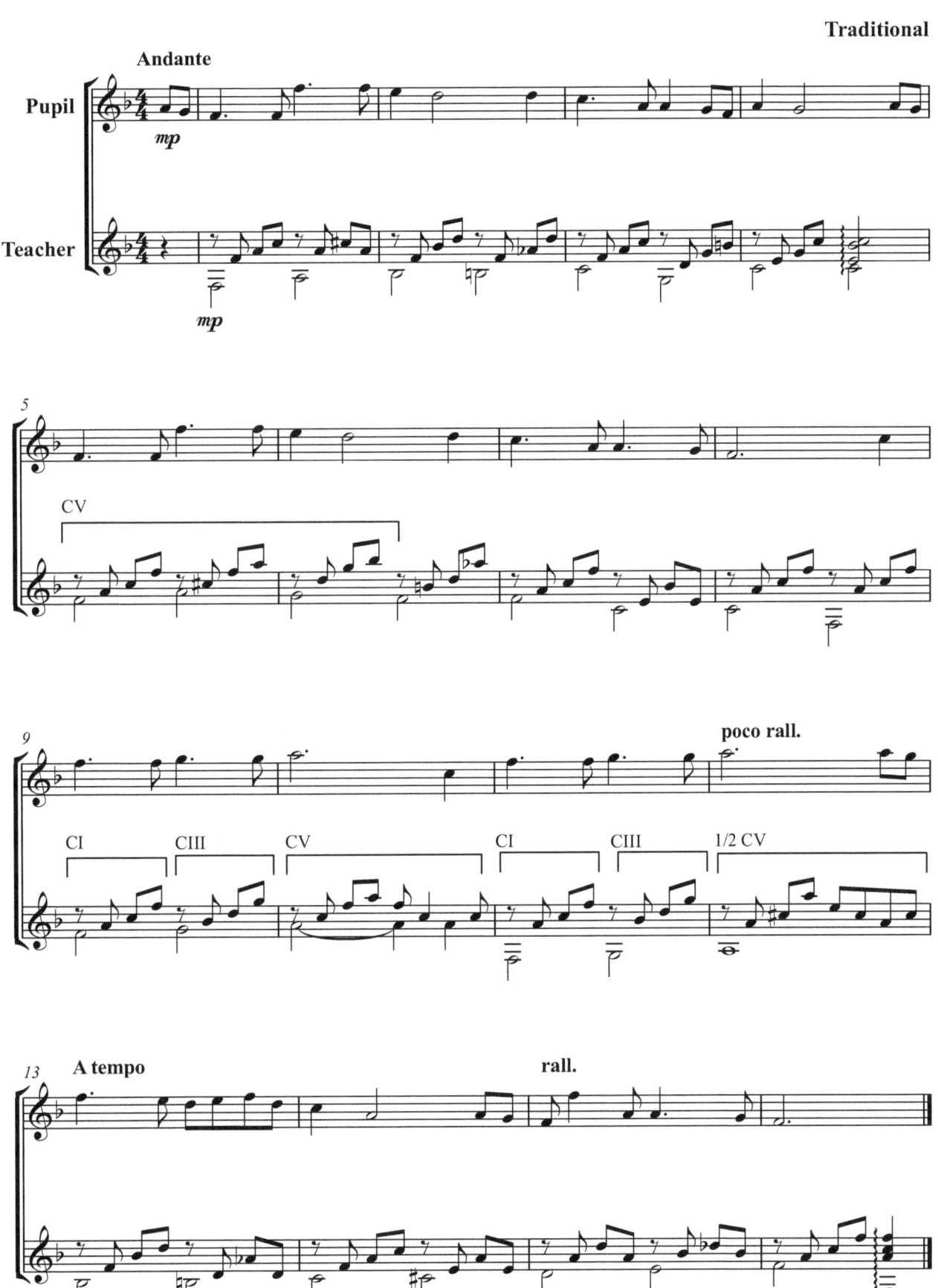